The First Lesson

A Novel

Nancy –
Enjoy the lesson –
Barbara R. Harrison

by

Barbara R. Harrison

The First Lesson

Acknowledgement

To my grandson, Justin Campbell, who is probably the real empath in my family.

INTRODUCTION

I CONSIDER MYSELF quite ordinary, and my life certainly didn't start out as anything remarkable. However, rather peculiar events occurring during the past year have transformed me into a person I'm just beginning to know.

I've been blessed—and cursed—with an awareness of something greater than I am that exists both *out there* as well as within me. It's the very essence of who I am, yet it is so much more.

Have you ever wondered where awareness occurs? Oh, in the mind surely, but then, where is Mind? The brain acts as the functioning organ by which we think. But the brain doesn't create thought, any more than it creates awareness.

I sometimes think awareness is a feeling. When I'm aware of love, I don't think love, I feel it. If I read something inspirational that makes me bob my head up and down in agreement, the acknowledgment comes from my heart, not my head.

For most people, the little fragments of understanding that make us say, "Aha!" happen in fits and starts, bits and pieces, over a lifetime. When we get to the end of our journey, I don't imagine we'll feel that we know it all. Just enough to make us wish we had learned more.

I wonder if someone like Jesus was born fully aware or if he, like the rest of us, came to his understanding of life gradually. Did he ever fully understand?

Did Mahatma Ghandi?

Or Mother Teresa?

Or Buddha?

I can't answer for them, but I can tell you how my own awareness of the truth - *my* truth - came about. It may not work for you, but that's okay. You have your own quest. Don’t forget to ask lots of questions. Just make sure you continue looking for your own answers.

After you've read my story, I hope you'll take a long look at your own life and realize awareness doesn't come from someplace outside yourself. It's within, and always has been. Seeking brings it forth.

Paxton Michaels

CHAPTER ONE

THE RESCUE

THE WOMAN STEERED through the driving rain, her windshield wipers working hard. Barely able to see, she rounded a curve on the winding road.

A horn blasted, shattering the air. Two cars met, metal screeching against metal. Both drivers struggled to keep their vehicles on the road. The Chevrolet Suburban righted itself after spinning, and ended up facing the direction from which it had come. The BMW flew off the road into open space, coming down hard on the side of the hill. It rolled once, then tore at the brush as it continued its descent, coming to rest at last at the base of a gnarled oak.

For a few moments, nothing could be heard but the pounding of the rain. The Chevy's headlights revealed black skid marks on the road. At the bottom of the hill, steam rose from the BMW's engine into a single beam of light. The other had been shattered.

Four young men exited the car onto Topanga as another vehicle bore down on them. They ran across the road to safety for fear the oncoming driver wouldn't see them in time. Straining brakes brought an old, beat up truck to a stop inches away from the disabled Chevrolet.

A man with a thick mustache leaned his head out of the window. He spoke in Spanish, but his meaning was obvious to the English-speaking men at the side of the road. "Get out of my way," he seemed to threaten, shaking his fist.

The Suburban's young driver took a chance. He hurried to the older man's truck and, with a smattering of nearly forgotten high school Spanish and many hand signals, he informed the driver of their plight.

Before too many minutes had passed, the banged-up truck had pushed the newer Suburban onto the shoulder. The truck driver provided flares so an additional accident could be avoided. After determining there was no cell phone reception on this stretch of the canyon, one of the younger men climbed into the truck's passenger seat, and they left to get help, the older man driving, the other to be sure someone understood, regardless of what language they encountered.

Another car and two motorcycles stopped. A woman and her teen-age son got out of a Toyota, and two men sporting black leather jackets and tight jeans dismounted their Harleys. Rain dripped down their necks and soaked their clothing.

Lightning streaked across the sky as the two bikers and the teen accompanied the three Chevy passengers down the hill, slipping and sliding in the mud. One held a flashlight, and tried to illuminate the path in front of them. They grasped at tree branches and underbrush, each secretly fearful they'd tumble down the hill and break a bone. The boy's mother remained on the road, waving a flare at on-coming cars. Some stopped to see what had happened. Others continued on their way, not wishing to be involved.

The men finally reached the wreck. Its hood had sprung, exposing the steaming engine to the rain. One of the cyclists tried the driver's door and found it locked. Another man found a rock and, after several failed attempts, smashed one of the rear door windows. He reached in and unlocked the front. While someone opened that door, he checked for a pulse in the woman's neck.

"She's still alive!" he shouted into the rain.

"Better not move her as long as the car doesn't burst into flames," said another. "She might have a broken back or neck."

"Yeah," said the Suburban's driver. "I wouldn't wanna get sued for making her a paraplegic or something."

"What's the difference? You're gonna be sued, anyway," one of his passengers said. "You ran her off the road."

"Shut up, Ben! It was an accident."

"Tell it to the judge, Marty."

The teenager hated conflict. He didn't want them to argue. "Shouldn't we check to see if she's bleeding? I know how to do a pressure bandage."

Distracted, the men checked out the woman's injuries.

"Looks like she bumped her head. Has a knot the size of a goose egg."

"Lucky she was wearin' a seat belt."

"I never wear a seat belt," one man bragged.

"Then, if it was you sitting here, you'd be dead."

Sirens pierced the night and two sheriff's cars, a fire truck and an ambulance pulled up to the edge of the road. Soon other men scrambled down the hill carrying black bags and a stretcher. A paramedic quickly examined the woman.

"Her leg is crushed. Looks like the crash pushed some of the engine parts into the car's interior. We'll have to pry her out of here."

Another checked her vital signs. “Cold, clammy, blood pressure low, minimal pulse. I’d bet anything she’s bleeding internally.” He spoke into a radio. “Bring a body mask down here.”

While men carried equipment to the rescuers, law-enforcement officers blocked traffic and ordered civilians back up the slippery hill where they could give their statements about what had happened.

The truck driver brought his passenger back to the scene and hung around hoping to hear that the woman was all right. Topanga Canyon was effectively closed to through traffic for three hours while rescue work continued.

The rain let up just about the time they pulled the woman from the car. Rescuers zipped her into a pressure suit and inflated it to slow the flow of blood to the extremities in case of internal bleeding. Then they immobilized her by strapping her to a board so they could carry her up the hill. Four men climbed gingerly to the road, two on each side of their precious cargo. A fifth held an IV line high as fluid dripped into her arm. By the time she had been loaded into the ambulance, the downpour stopped. Paramedics radioed ahead to the hospital so a team of doctors and nurses would be waiting for their arrival.

A paramedic radioed ahead to the hospital. "Name’s Paxton Michaels, 34 years old, lives in the Palisades. Looks like a fractured tibia and a head injury. The leg’s pretty bad. Can't tell what's going on inside. Might be some internal injuries."

As soon as the ambulance doors were secured, its driver started the engine, and they rushed off into the darkness, sirens wailing.

The teenager let his mother enfold him in her arms, even though he was taller than she. "I don't want her to die, Mom."

The woman comforted her son. "You did what you could, Eric. Now it's up to God."

"And a good medical team that I'll probably have to pay for whether she lives or not," the Chevy's driver added.

CHAPTER TWO

IN THE BEGINNING

IT BEGAN ON a typical, rather ordinary day.

"Alex!" I called from the bottom of the stairs. "You're going to be late for school again."

My daughter came out of her room and looked over the railing.

"Who cares, Mom? Graduation's next week. If I haven't made it by now, forget it."

I closed my eyes and listened to the jangling of my nerves. She had been like this for weeks, her verbal barbs tossed like daggers into my heart. What happened to the babe that smelled so good when freshly bathed and thought I was her sun and moon? How had she left that world of wonder a child sees with each new experience and traversed into the cynical, angry realm she inhabited today? I started up the stairs, knuckles whitening under the pressure of gripping the wrought iron hand rail. *Calm down, Paxton*, I thought. *You're the adult, right?*

"I don't appreciate your attitude, young lady. Your father and I worked hard to get you this far."

She laughed and twisted the knife. "*Dad* worked hard. It's his money that paid for the private schools and tutors. *I* worked hard so I can graduate—with honors, I might remind you. You just schlepped me back and forth to school."

Cruelty poured from my daughter's mouth like water from a spring. I felt defeated, because Alex only echoed my own thoughts these past few months. I gave up the fight and retreated into the mundane.

"All right, Alex. Come down when you're dressed. I'll have the car ready. You can eat cold toast on the way."

I walked to the kitchen and poured a cup of coffee. My husband stood at the counter, sorting through some papers, looking great. He worked out often, determined to beat the aging process. He had so much exercise equipment, the bonus room off our bedroom looked like a gymnasium.

"Robert, we haven't had much chance to talk lately. How about lunch one of these days?"

"Hm?" he answered, obviously distracted by his reading. "Sure. One of these days."

He put the papers in his Hartman briefcase, snapped the lock, and then turned to give me his full attention.

"Why do you let her get away with that crap?"

"Let her? How can I stop her when she has you for a role model?"

"Once again, it turns out to be Robert's fault." I cringed under his sarcasm. "Did you ever stop to think people treat you the way you want to be treated?"

I winced, having wondered the same thing. Nevertheless, I went on the defensive. "That's the stupidest thing you've ever said. Why in the world would I want the treatment you dish out?"

"Okay, wrong choice of words," Robert said. His dark eyes flashed angry sparks. "Let's try the way you *expect* to be treated."

I rolled my eyes in disgust.

"I mean it, Paxton. I saw a television interview with a mugger. He said he watches for people who act like victims. The way they walk, their eyes darting like frightened birds. The scared ones—those are the targets."

"Are you implying I'm afraid of you?"

"Jesus! You don't get it, do you?"

He slid his brief case off the tile and headed for the door. "I won't be home for dinner." The screen slammed behind him.

Lately, I *had* been afraid. Not of Robert, although I hated when he got angry and often lied to protect myself. When did things change? I used to be able to tell him anything. Everything.

I suppose my fears began when Robert started working late, often sleeping on the couch in his office. At least, that's where he said he slept. He kept a change of clothing there, and a razor and toothbrush.

On Saturdays and Sundays, he had a standing foursome at the country club and I, like so many other wives I knew, rarely saw my husband before dinner on the weekends.

It hadn't always been like that. After we married in the little Methodist Church on Spring Street, Robert doted on me, spending every spare minute demonstrating his love. I was only eighteen and thrilled with catching this handsome, older, college graduate.

His father financed our honeymoon in Hawaii and made the proper introductions so Robert could get in on the ground floor with A & M Credit Software. He quickly worked his way up from salesman to head his department, then took the company's business into other countries as its international sales manager. Now, he enjoyed the prestige of being Senior Veepee, next in line for the presidency.

I worked as a receptionist when we got married, but Alex came along ten months later. Robert told me, "You don't need to work. I make enough money to support us. Besides, I don't want my daughter brought up by some nanny who doesn't speak English."

I agreed, as I always did with Robert, although jumping feet first into motherhood threw a damper on the hot flames of my desire to study art at UCLA.

By the time Alex entered kindergarten, my role in life had been established. Robert convinced me I'd never have any use for a degree—that I could depend on him to take care of me for the rest of my life.

"Even if something happens to me," he said, "I have enough insurance so you'll never have to work."

Secretly, I took classes in watercolor and decorated our home with my own paintings. I do pretty decent stuff, and I'm really happy with about one out of every ten canvases. My best friend, Moira Plunkett, is always trying to persuade me to exhibit them someplace, but Robert said I'd be setting myself up for disappointment.

While I sipped my coffee, I stared at a two foot long abstract of pink and white roses I'd hung over the kitchen entrance.

Alex came into the room dressed in jeans and a tee shirt that read, *Ask me! I might say yes.*

"You're not going to school in that," I said.

"Mother! You're so dull. All the kids wear things like this. It's fashionable."

I tried reasoning with my daughter. "The wrong person might take you up on your offer."

"If it's the wrong person, I'll say no. Besides, I don't have time to change. If we leave right now, I can make it before the bell rings."

Alex picked up a piece of cold, buttered wheat toast from a plate on the kitchen table and sprinkled sugar on it.

"For quick energy," she said, eyeing my reaction. "C'mon Mom."

Feeling defeated once again, I sighed and followed Alex to the car. It almost seemed as if I didn't care any more. About anything.

"I'll drive," Alex said, plucking the keys from my hand. "I need the practice so I can get my license."

I slid in on the passenger's side and stared straight ahead while my daughter maneuvered out of the driveway and sped down the street.

"Slow down, honey."

"Geeze, Mom, you must be getting old. Remember when we had that big, old, Dodge station wagon and you'd put a cardboard box in the back? I'd get in and then you'd whip around corners really fast, and I'd slide around the back like crazy."

I couldn't help smiling. Back then, I still loved the element of risk in things I did.

"That was before seat belt laws, kiddo. And before your Uncle Keith got killed drag racing."

"Oh, for Christ's sake, Mom, I'm not racing. Look..." She pointed to the speedometer. "Only ten miles over the limit."

"Lucky for me, we're more than a few blocks from home already. Statistics show that's where most auto accidents happen. And watch your language."

Alex shot me a look. "If you're trying to make me feel guilty, don't bother. I haven't hit anything yet."

"Key word. Yet. You've only had your learner's permit for a few weeks."

"Dad doesn't rag on me like you do."

"Good. From now on, you only drive when he's in the car."

"Aw, Mom."

Alex pulled the car into the Palisades High School parking lot. She honked her horn at three teenagers getting out of a car and waved. They returned her greeting.

"Think they're impressed?" I asked. I couldn't keep a hint of sarcasm out of my voice.

"They'll be more impressed when I have a car of my own. Dad's gonna buy me one as soon as I pass my driver's test."

Another of Robert's little secrets. "I don't recall discussing this with your father."

"Since when does he discuss anything with you? He's the decision maker in this family."

I stared at my daughter, suddenly appalled at what I'd done. "My God, Alex. I am so sorry."

"For what?"

"What kind of role model have I been? My mother, and now me. How could I not have seen it? The sins of the mother are visited onto her children even unto the third generation."

Alex pulled into a handicapped space. "You're talking weird." She shook her head, gathered up her books, and scooted out of the car. "Bye, Mom. Pick me up at five. I have graduation rehearsal after school." She slammed the door.

"Alex!" I yelled, but she turned and ran through the gate just as the bell rang.

I exited the car, got back in on the driver's side, and positioned myself behind the wheel. *She's lying*, I thought. *When I graduated, rehearsal occurred during school hours.*

I waved half-heartedly at another tardy teen, one of Alex's friends, and sighed. "I give up. Okay, car, get me out of here."

All I could think about while I drove was how I'd provided such a bad example for my little girl. She grew up seeing me give in to Robert on every front. I conceded to him on both important and trivial matters. Would she emulate me in her own relationships? "Good Lord," I said, realizing my mother had also taught me well.

At home, I created a work schedule that would keep me busy all day if I wanted. My long list of chores began with washing and ironing, and cleaning the tile grout in all three bathrooms. Not that the grout looked dirty. Robert just liked it sparkling white.

When I finished the tile in the master bathroom, I happened to look in the mirror and caught a glimpse of a frazzled-looking woman wearing a frown. Deep lines creased the area where my brows drew together above my nose.

"You look terrible," I told my reflection, attempting to smooth the furrows with my forefinger.

I glanced at my wrist. Eleven o'clock. Suddenly, I had an idea. Why not have that lunch with Robert today? Surprise him.

In the early days of our marriage, I would occasionally dress in something sexy with nothing on beneath but skin and catch Robert in his office just before lunch. Maybe, I thought, just maybe I can bring back some of the passion. For all of his faults, I still loved him.

I put the bottle of bleach and worn toothbrush I'd been working with under the sink, stripped, and turned on the water in the shower. Two hours to get ready. Robert's a creature of habit. Lunch precisely at one.

Later, I emerged from the house, hair squeaky clean and swinging free, just brushing my shoulders. Braless nipples showed beneath my blue linen chemise, and thigh high nylons caressed my legs like silk. My stilletto heels clicked a rhythmic beat on the pavement as I walked to the car. I felt good. For the first time in weeks, the roses in my cheeks had nothing to do with skillfully applied blush.

A short time later, I pulled the family SUV in beside Robert's Ferrari. I walked the short distance to the elevator and rode up in silence beside a middle-aged man who waggled his eyebrows at me. He got off one floor before mine and I called after him. "You ought to be ashamed of yourself."

The man turned red and edged out of sight as the doors closed, leaving me chuckling alone.

Robert's penthouse office seemed quiet. His secretary had apparently gone to lunch having shoved her chair neatly under the desk and turned off the computer's monitor.

Good. We'd be completely alone.

I placed my hand on the door handle, then stopped to read the brass name plate. Robert W. Michaels, III. A sense of pride ran through me. That's my husband, I thought. Successful, handsome, fit and trim. Young to be in this position. No matter that he's been acting so dictatorial. I still wanted my marriage to work.

Admitting that, I pushed on the latch. Locked. I tapped on the mahogany. "Robert?"

From inside, I heard a woman's voice. "Oh, my God."

"Who is it?" Robert yelled.

"It's me, Paxton."

Suddenly, I didn't want him to open the door. I knew if he did, my whole life would change. I turned and ran to the elevator, punching the down button with desperate jabs. Only one car came to the Penthouse floor, and I felt sure it was probably stuck open on one of the lower levels.

Robert opened his office. "What are you doing here? You should have called."

I turned around and saw my husband standing in the doorway. Behind him, a beautiful blonde stood tucking her blouse into a pencil slim skirt. I recognized her from last year's Christmas party. Nikki something. Funny how you notice things in times of crisis. The skirt was a wraparound in an odd shade of green with a flat, pearl button at the waistband. Except for her tousled hair, she looked every bit the part of a young, female executive as she slipped into her matching jacket with matching pearl button.

"We talked about having lunch," I said, feeling stupid. "I-I-I...."

"Stop stuttering, Paxton."

I took a deep breath. "I wanted to surprise you. I guess I did."

The woman pushed past Robert, but stood near him.

I saw pity on her face. Nothing could have angered me more. Robert laid a hand on the woman's arm. "Let me talk with my wife alone, Nikki. I'll call you later."

Nikki turned to leave but paused long enough to say, "It's not what you think, Mrs. Michaels."

I watched in a daze as Robert apparently changed his mind about Nikki leaving. He reached out and halted her progress.

While I looked on in horror, Robert shook his head. "No more lies," he told me. "It *is* what you think, Paxton. This is Nikki Oliver, our company comptroller."

"Is she the reason you've been keeping late hours every night?"

"Yes."

"You're having an affair?"

"It's more than that. I love her."

"No!" I shouted. "You can't. You love me. Me! I'm your wife."

"You and I haven't loved each other for a long time. We've only been roommates for months now."

His words stabbed painfully into my heart. While I disagreed with him, I couldn't deny that our relationship had grown more and more distant in the past year.

"I've been everything you wanted me to be," I pleaded. I was whining and hated myself for it. My voice sounded hoarse as I struggled to hold back tears. "I keep your house the way you like it. I don't work because you asked me not to. I roll your socks the way you prefer them and press your boxer shorts and bake homemade desserts and throw parties for your clients." I ran out of breath. "What more could you want? I'd have given it. I *will* give it."

"What I want, you can't give. It isn't in you. I need a partner, someone who shares my ambitions and has ideas of her own, not a frightened little girl who gives in to me at every turn." He must have seen how defeated I felt. "To be fair, I didn't know that's what I wanted until I met Nikki. She's shown me just how good things can be."

"Fair! I gave up being me so you could do and be what you wanted. What about my life? What about me?"

Robert grabbed my shoulders and shook me. "You're hysterical, Paxton. When you calm down, you'll realize this is for the best. Now, you can pursue your own interests. Sell those silly paintings you like to do or something. One of these days, you'll thank me."

I straightened my back and pulled loose from his grasp. "If only you knew how ridiculous and condescending that sounds." I turned to Nikki. "Your turn will come. There'll be a day when you aren't enough, either."

My prediction was a thinly veiled attempt to get even. I saw she didn't believe me.

"Don't bother to come home." I spat the words at him. "I'll make arrangements to send your things wherever you want."

"Paxton, that's crazy. That house is as much my home as it is yours. We can discuss what we're going to do this evening. Of course, if *you* wish to leave, I'll make sure you have enough money to settle in some place."

A sneer twisted my face. Or maybe it was just the effort to keep from crying. At any rate, I knew it was time to get out of there when the elevator door opened. I got in and turned to stare at them. Robert put his arm around Nikki again. I couldn't help myself. I gave them the finger just before the door closed.

I'm not sure how I made it home. I scarcely remember anything about the trip except that I cried all the way. I vacillated between anger and self-pity so many times, I confused myself.

When I went into the house, I slammed the door hard behind me. That felt good. So good, I opened and slammed it again. And again. It was enough to stop my crying. Then I took a lead crystal vase from the narrow table in the entry way and threw it against the wall. The vase shattered, leaving a lovely gouge in the plaster.

I stepped over the broken shards of glass and went to the kitchen for a broom, ashamed at my loss of control. There was no sense leaving my mess where Alex might step on it when she came home. I toyed with the idea of dumping the pieces in Robert's favorite chair. However, reason won out. I was always reasonable. The glass ended up in the trash.

I walked around the house in a daze, examining memories. There was the rocking chair we'd purchased at a funky, second hand shop on our first anniversary. Robert had wanted to toss it when we redecorated, but I couldn't part with it. It looked out of place with the art deco style Robert preferred, and I realized it was the only piece of furniture I truly loved.

A statue of some long-forgotten fertility god sat on the marble fireplace mantle. We picked that up in Peru, the only vacation I'd chosen, after reading Shirley Maclaine's *Out on A Limb*. How disappointing! I had expected to sense something there, maybe even develop some latent psychic ability. It never happened. The only things I got out of the trip were mosquito bites and sunburn.

I touched the frame that held our wedding picture. How could this be happening? I had believed the fairy tale of happily ever after. Grimm never wrote about how the prince left the princess for another woman. The tears started again.

An hour later, my body still shook with great, wrenching sobs. I decided I'd never be happy again. Even if Robert changed his mind and stayed, it wouldn't be the same. I'd always be suspicious and untrusting. My life, as I knew it, was over.

In the bathroom, I patted my red, swollen eyes with a cold, wet cloth. The face staring back from the mirror didn't even look like me. An idea formed in the back of my mind. Wouldn't Robert be sorry if he came home and found me dead?

I opened the medicine cabinet and looked for something lethal. Half a bottle of generic ibuprofen. Would that be enough to do the job? Add an overdose of birth control pills and some out-of-date Tylenol ® with codeine left over from the time Robert broke his ankle skiing.

Turning on the water, I filled a glass, then flipped open the top of the ibuprofen bottle and poured the capsules into my palm.

Fear gripped me like a vise. I couldn't do it. For one thing, it might be Alex who found me, not her father. I wouldn't do that to her. Not only that, I suddenly decided I had no intention of letting Robert's affair end my life.

But I didn't know what kind of life it would be now.

Some strong instinct stirred deep inside me. I applied a little make-up to replace what had washed off, changed to blue jeans, tee-shirt, and tennies, and tied a sweatshirt around my waist. It was time to go for a walk on the beach.

Living near the Pacific Ocean has its advantages. Ever since I was a little girl, I have felt closer to God walking along the seashore on a sandy beach than I ever did in a church. Sometimes, during the rigid worship services of my childhood, I'd wonder why people called our church the House of God.

"God doesn't live here," I explained to my mother with an eight-year-old's wisdom. "He's in the woods and out on the ocean. No building is big enough to keep God inside."

A soap-washed mouth rewarded that observation.

After that, I kept my thoughts to myself, but I still feel the power of God in the roar of the ocean. I see its majesty in a snow covered mountain and feel the serenity of a Master Presence while walking beneath the branches of a redwood. On that terrible day, I escaped to where I could commune with my source. I drove down Chattaqua Boulevard to Highway One and headed north until I got to Westward Beach. I followed the road to the end and parked.

The waves rose high and a few hardy souls braved brisk temperatures, testing their surfing skills. Other than that, I was practically the only person on the beach. I walked to Zuma and back, then sat on the sand, letting the wind whip my hair while I went over the events of the day. Tears came and went many times while I sat, and I waited for the moment when I knew everything would be all right. That moment never came. I simply got angrier and yelled at God.

"Why did you do this to me? I deserve better than this!"

A seal raised its head out of the water, staring as if I had accused him of something.

Later, I confessed loudly, "I don't even believe in you any more. If you were real, you wouldn't let this happen."

Finally, just as the sun sank below the horizon and my fingers and toes warned me of impending frostbite, I cried, "Help me, please! Show me what to do. Whatever it takes. Just give me a sign."

With that, I shivered and trudged back to my waiting car. I still wasn't ready to go home and face Robert, although I wondered if Alex had found a ride home. I'd feel guilty later. She'd make sure of that.

At Topanga Canyon, I turned left and stepped on the gas, taking the curves at top speed, ignoring the raindrops that spattered my windshield. My senses raced, remembering how Robert used to tease me about my reckless driving. After my brother, Keith, died in an auto accident, I slowed down. But I was still good behind the wheel.

Just before reaching the tunnel, the rain became a downpour. In California, it rains so seldom, drivers don't know how to handle a car on roads slick with wet grime. My mechanic once explained how a car can hydroplane if brakes are incorrectly applied. That must be what happened when the Suburban coming from the opposite direction skidded around the curve and crossed the line. Its driver corrected the skid, too late to avoid side-swiping me. I turned the steering wheel hard, but my vehicle didn't respond. I just kept sliding sideways over the edge of the road. Suddenly, I was airborne. Someone screamed and since I was the only one in the car, it must have been me. The last thing I remember before blacking out is a gnarled oak that seemed to hurtle toward me.

CHAPTER THREE

LIFE AFTER DEATH

I OPENED MY eyes and stretched, feeling myself all over to see if anything had broken. Not even a scratch, apparently. No aches or pains. It was dark. At first, I couldn't see anything. Then, from a distance, I spotted a light.

Must be a rescue party, I figured, and started walking toward it. Or at least, I thought I was walking, until I noticed how fast I was traveling.

I picked up speed and propelled toward the light which got brighter as I neared the source.

My God, I thought, *I must be dead. This is just like I read it would be. Go into the light.*

Tree branches rushed by and I reached out, desperately trying to stop my forward movement. "Wait!" I shouted. "I asked for help. I didn't want to be put out of my misery!" I couldn't stand knowing Robert would suppose I'd flown off the road on purpose. What a boost for his ego.

My mind screamed. How will Alex make it through life without her mother? She's on the verge of womanhood, facing her first year of college, nearly two years younger than the rest of her class. She needs me.

My thoughts flew back to the day Alex was born. Robert had been so disappointed; he wanted a son. Robert, Jr. He argued for Roberta, but settled for Alex, the closest he could come to a boy's name with my agreement.

As I rushed toward the light, I thought this must be what it's like to be born. Being propelled down a dark tunnel into the light. Perhaps this, too, was a birth of some kind.

My thoughts had calmed me down and, with the calm, my forward movement slowed to a less desperate momentum.

Ahead, I spotted the shadowy outline of a male figure superimposed over the brightness. A moment later, I found myself standing in front of the most beautiful man I'd ever seen. My heart, if I still had one, jittered. How funny, I thought. Just moments ago, I was devastated over losing Robert and here I am attracted to this gorgeous, dark haired, doe-eyed man. Italian from the looks of it.

The man placed his hands on my shoulders and gazed into my eyes. "Welcome," he said.

"To heaven?"

The man laughed. "Heaven is wherever you choose it to be."

I looked around at the brilliantly colored scenery. Trees overburdened with leaves seemed greener, flowers blossomed with an array of colors unlike any I'd ever seen.

"This is too wonderful to be hell. So it must be heaven or... Where am I?"

"Does it matter? You are just here."

Not quite the answer I sought. "And you are?"

"You may call me David. I'm your teacher."

He put his arms around me and hugged. In that instant, I knew what love was. Never had I felt so completely cherished. Without saying a word, he conveyed honor and respect, kindness and devotion. I basked in the feeling, awed by his presence.

This had to be a dream. "All this is rather new to me and, so far, I'm hopelessly confused. Do you suppose we could start over?"

"Good idea," David said. "Why don't we walk together."

He linked his arm with mine, and we started off through the forest. It seemed so natural to be walking along at his side. I knew I should ask questions, be more curious about what was happening. Yet it felt so right, just letting things take place.

Birds struck up a melodious symphony.

"How beautiful they sing," I said.

"Yes, it's a background of harmony. If you prefer silence, you can ask them to stop."

"I can do that?"

David nodded.

"What if I prefer silence and you don't?"

"Then we both shall be satisfied."

"I don't understand."

David explained. "Everything is done according to one's preference. And all things happen simultaneously. Would you like to experiment? Imagine yourself in a quiet place."

I closed my eyes and pictured myself floating in a canoe on a still, glass-surfaced lake. On a nearby island, trees hung thick with moss, the earth rich, black loam. I listened and heard nothing but my own intake and outflow of breath. I opened my eyes and found we were sitting in the scene I'd imagined.

"Wow!"

"Try again with something different."

I saw myself in my favorite place, a rocky beach in Big Sur, California, listening to the crash of waves on the shore. Immediately, we were there.

"I think I'm going to like this place. Can I do this at will?"

"Of course. But you'll be too busy to bother."

I wasn't sure I wanted to know what I'd be too busy doing. David continued. "Imagination is the key to creating a life of preference."

"I wish I could have done that before."

"You always could. You just didn't know it."

I didn't believe him. "Do you mean to tell me all I had to do was imagine my husband loving me instead of another woman and he'd do it?"

"Not exactly."

I would soon find out those were David's two favorite words.

"So *exactly* what do you mean?"

"Every person is gifted with full choice over what to accept or reject in their lives. This includes choice about our experiences."

Isn't that kind of like what Robert told me this morning? What did he say? *Did you ever stop to think people treat you the way you expect to be treated?*

I spied David watching me and felt like a little kid caught in a lie. It seemed as if he could read my thoughts.

"I can," he confirmed, "but only when you let yourself open up to allow it."

"I guess I'd better keep close watch over what I'm thinking."

David smiled. "You're absolutely right. It's always a good idea to be aware of your thoughts and provide them direction. Your subconscious mind takes everything you think or say literally."

"Like that time I wanted to quit my job as a volunteer aide at my daughter's school? I continued working even though I didn't want to, thinking there wasn't anyone else to take my place. Then they 'fired' me, saying they needed someone bilingual. And there *was* another person who took my place, really soon. Kind of like that?"

David grinned. "Kind of," he echoed. "Listen, would you like something to eat?"

He plucked a red apple from a nearby tree. Sudden, ravenous hunger pangs gripped my stomach. I remembered I hadn't eaten since breakfast early that morning.

"In my daughter's words, this is weird," I said, biting into my apple. "If I'm dead, why do I need something to eat?" Juice ran down my chin. "This is delicious."

"Perhaps you still live."

"Life after death. Okay, I'm convinced. But it isn't at all like I imagined." So much for David's theory about imagination. "Am I missing something here?"

"The pieces will all fall into place over the next few days. For now, let us simply say, you are here to learn your reason for being, Paxton Michaels." He took my hand. "Come, I'll show you the way."

We seemed to move through a fog. Every now and then I caught a glimpse of other pairs of people sitting or walking just as we were doing.

"Who are they?"

"Others like you."

"And like you?"

"Yes."

Who was this man? Was he some kind of superior being?

An older man passed by. He touched my arm, leaving me with a warm feeling. "David's an angel."

Had *he* read my thoughts, too?

"Is everybody around here a mind reader?" I asked.

"Only when you allow it," the old man answered and moved on.

I turned to David. "You said something like that, too. I'm not consciously letting people into my thoughts. In fact, I don't think I like it at all. How can I stop them from listening in?"

"By stopping the flow of energy that emanates from your heart."

"That sounds scary. I'm not sure I'd care to learn that."

David smiled. "Good. However, you have complete freedom of choice. We can work on it later if you decide."

We sat on a carpet of grass under an oak which spread its limbs above us like a canopy.

“So you’re a teacher,” I said, making conversation. “Why?”

David had a bemused look on his face. "Here, we serve out of love. Through service, we grow."

I shook my head and sighed, lifted my apple and took another bite. My entire being exploded with its exquisite taste. I felt as if the spirit of the fruit entered my soul, becoming a part of me. The apple seemed to be fulfilling its destiny, continuing life through me.

"This is..." I stopped, at a loss for words.

"Delicious?"

"More than that. It's like I became the apple or it became part of me. I wanted to beg its pardon for eating it, but I felt—this sounds silly—like the apple forgave me."

"Ah! You have experienced your oneness with what our Source created."

"Whatever that means."

"I'll explain by using a time-honored axiom. You're familiar with the ocean?"

"Of course. I spend a lot of time near it."

"The ocean is made up of millions and millions of water drops. Any one of these drops contains within it all of the properties of the ocean. It is wet, salty, contains minerals, is comprised of hydrogen and oxygen, atoms and molecules. It is part of the ocean. At the same time, all of the ocean is contained in an individual drop. Do you understand?"

"I think so."

"You have within you all the qualities of the bigger picture, as well. You are intelligent, healthy, capable of experiencing love, joy, harmony, peace and so much more." He smiled and spread his arms wide. "Now do you see?"

"Not really."

An exasperated look crossed David's face, but only for a moment. "Just as the drop is one with the ocean, so are you one with the One. Everything that the One is, you are. At the same time, all of the One is individualized in you."

"I presume you're talking about God."

David just smiled.

What an amazing concept to digest. I grew up thinking of God as an old man sitting on a throne up in heaven or at least somewhere way off in the ether, and that human beings looked like they do because they were made in his image. The notion that we think because God is thought, love because God is love, and are healthy because God is wholeness would take some getting used to. I liked the idea.

"If I understand correctly, you're saying, first of all, that God is bigger than the male image I've assigned him to be. He's not, well, a man."

"The One is all men, and women, too."

I’d have to ponder that one later. "Then what do I call him? He-She? Father-Mother?"

"The One cares not what name is used. It is known by many names—God, Allah, Buddha, Father-Mother, the Source, the Force. You may choose."

"You said God is all men. How could Hitler or Attila the Hun be considered anything close to God?"

"Ah, you begin your lesson with hard questions," David said. "Yet, the answer is easy. Humans are given the choice of using their God qualities as they wish. Some use them in what may seem to be inappropriate ways. But it is not for us to judge."

I shook my head in disbelief, feeling *quite* judgmental. “Their choices were evil!”

“Good and evil are perceptions.”

“Maybe so, but I still can’t justify the actions of despots and tyrants.” I narrowed my eyes at him. "I certainly wouldn't have done things that way."

"Perhaps one day you will find a way to change things—or, instead, see the wisdom of doing them God's way."

David rose and it seemed natural to stand with him. He took both my hands in his and, again, I felt his powerful love.

"We have had enough questions for today," he said. "It is time to rest. Tomorrow we will begin your lessons in earnest. Follow me."

"Am I supposed to sleep? I didn't think I'd need sleep here."

"It is best that you do. You will discover the reason later," David said.

"Must you speak in riddles?" I asked.

"The ancient Druids taught their philosophy through riddles."

"I didn't know that," I said, distracted from my original question. Perhaps that was his purpose.

"What is sharper than the sword?" he asked.

"A razor?"

"No, understanding." David raised his eyebrows, waiting to see if I followed his reasoning. When I nodded, he asked, "What is whiter than snow?"

I sifted through the information my memory held, trying to find an answer. "Purity."

"That's an excellent answer, but a better one might be truth."

I didn't necessarily agree with him, but I had warmed up to the game. "Ask me another."

"What is blacker than the raven?"

This time I had a ready answer, but he gave me his version before I could respond.

"Death," he said.

"I would have said evil."

"You're very good. Isn't it interesting that we have both chosen answers to this last question which do not exist?"

"Is this another riddle?" I asked.

"It certainly wasn't meant to be. Life goes on in non-physical form when the soul is done with the body. And you'll recall what I said about Hitler and Attila."

I must have looked puzzled. David smiled and gently suggested that I get some rest. "You may use the stillness of night to ponder what you have learned."

With that, he turned and left. My head filled with things that I never got around to asking because one question answered led to so many others.

Suddenly I ached with weariness. I closed my eyes and yawned, longing for a bed. When I opened them again, I found myself standing alone in a room where I felt completely at peace. A king-sized bed beckoned to me. A nightgown hung on the bedpost, and I slipped into it, grateful to get out of my mud-caked jeans and dirty tennis shoes. I had nearly forgotten how I got there.

I fell asleep the minute my head hit the pillow.

CHAPTER FOUR

THE FIRST LESSON

I WOKE WITH a start, then settled back on my pillow and stretched, allowing my body to waken an inch at a time. Gauzy curtains fluttered at the window where sunlight streamed through, and a gentle breeze kissed my face. Words from a song knocked at my memory, something about plenty of sunshine heading my way. The whole scene seemed to promise a wonderful day.

As my feet touched the floor, I heard a light tapping of knuckles on my door.

"Good morning, Paxton Michaels. Would you like some breakfast?"

I donned a robe and opened the door. David stood there balancing a tray, smiling.

"Come in," I said, inviting him with a gesture. "You have perfect timing."

"All time is perfect," he said. "I hope you like fruit."

"Somehow, I feel you already know that's my favorite breakfast."

He uncovered the tray to reveal thin slices of cantaloupe, honeydew, watermelon, thick chunks of crunchy green and red apples, and a banana, all garnished with seedless grapes and sprigs of mint. I bit into a grape and knew I'd been given quite a gift.

"Why do things taste so much better here?"

"Perhaps your expectations are higher?" David said. "Or maybe it's because our trees and plants have never known the need for pesticides."

"Pesticides keep away insects and worms that destroy crops," I said, defending my world. "Farmers could lose everything without them."

His response was gentle. "I didn't meant to sound judgmental. We just don't need such things. There's plenty for everyone here—including insects and worms."

"It amazes me you'd have bugs here."

"Why? They're all part of creation. Everything has a place and a purpose." Before I could respond, he pointed. "If you'd like, you may dress when you've eaten."

At the foot of my bed, a soft, white outfit lay neatly folded. The flared pants and loose top looked to be exactly my size. Who had brought them in the night? And where were my clothes?

David answered my thoughts. "The outfit you wore yesterday is clean. You'll find it in the dresser should you prefer to wear your own things."

He left so quietly, I wasn't sure he had even been there, except that I had a platter of food and a huge glass of freshly squeezed orange juice in front of me. I ate my fill and decided to dress in the comfortable outfit that looked much like the one David wore. The moment I finished and patted my hair into place, another knock sounded.

David entered at my bidding.

"Are you prepared to begin your first lesson?"

"I guess so. Where do we start?"

"Perhaps by taking a walk," he said.

I followed him outside. We strolled down a path that circled a small lake. The scent of flowering plants reached my nostrils, and beauty assailed my senses from every angle.

"This place reminds me of the Self Realization Center on Sunset Boulevard," I told him.

"How wonderful! A place to realize your Self. Which is exactly what you shall be doing the next few days."

"It's strange. I'm already feeling like I know myself better than I did just a few hours ago. I can't explain it, but I don't seem as concerned about… well, about things in general."

"We do have a different perspective here, undoubtedly because we don't color our circumstances with judgment. Situations and conditions simply are."

"I think I know what you mean. Or perhaps I don't. Not on a personal level, anyway." I grew silent for a few moments, trying to put this new found understanding into words. "My husband loves another woman, and my daughter thinks I've abandoned her emotionally. Are you telling me I shouldn't judge Robert for cheating on me? Or myself for causing my daughter pain?"

"Not exactly."

"Not exactly? How *exactly* should I think?"

"It's not my job to tell you how to think, only to point out there is another way of looking at things. You may choose."

My frustration exploded. "Oh, for heaven's sake, will you stop with that choice stuff! I didn't choose to have Robert fooling around with that tight-assed…. Sorry. That female who's closer to my daughter's age than mine."

David looked amused. "Didn't you?"

"Of course not. How could you even insinuate such a thing?"

David took my hand in his and again I felt his deep caring. His touch calmed me.

"Many times," he said, "we set ourselves up for certain things to happen, based on how we feel about ourselves. How long has it been since you truly felt you were a worthwhile person?"

I couldn't deny it had been a long time. How subtly it had begun, years ago when Robert learned to play golf, for instance. The game became more important than being with me. "Okay, so I don't feel adorable. But that's because things happened to make me feel that way."

"Really?"

"You're exasperating, David. Yes, really."

"Think about it, Paxton."

My first instinct was to blame Robert for everything. I thought back to earlier times, even before we married. Often, the thought crossed my mind that I didn't deserve Robert. Even more frequently, I worried that he wouldn't want me forever, and fear turned me into the good little wife who did everything Robert's way. Admitting that, I also conceded I must have bored Robert to death.

"So, if I act like I don't deserve his love, he picks up on it. Is that what you're saying?"

"In a way. He, too, contributes to the total picture, of course. If Robert also feels undeserving, you may overwhelm him with your emotion, and he looks elsewhere to affirm his own low self-esteem."

"Then, in our neediness, we could have attracted each other."

"Exactly."

"Well that's a relief. I got an *exactly* out of you. But it doesn't make me feel any better, and I still can't condone his making love to that woman in his office. Frankly, if I attracted Robert for those reasons, then I'm as guilty as he is. If I'd been different, maybe this wouldn't have happened."

"There is nothing to feel guilty about. You simply made choices. Now you can make new choices."

"And if I choose to win him back?" I talked like I was still alive.

"You might be disappointed to have him."

I nodded, reluctantly, recalling a friend who pined for her ex-husband for nearly ten years. Her whole focus was on trying to get him back. When she finally succeeded, he moved in with all his old baggage, and I don't mean luggage. Within three months, she was working to get him out of her home and her life. She couldn't stand the man and wondered why she ever bothered to mourn his leaving. He hadn't changed a bit, but she had.

David continued, echoing my thoughts. "Real choice comes with changing yourself, not changing another or his actions. Robert may choose to return to you, but if neither of you changes inwardly, being together could be just as miserable as living apart. Let us begin our lesson, and you may see what I mean."

We sat on plush grass beneath the spreading branches of a huge elm. Colorful birds chirped overhead. A bee buzzed past my ear and landed on my knee. For the first time I could remember, I didn't panic. Normally, I would have yelled and swatted at the creature, probably enraging it to the point of attack. We watched the bee which, in turn, seemed to be inspecting us. A moment later, it flew off.

"Amazing!" I said. "I wasn't afraid."

"Most fear is learned. It is a powerful emotion that increases in strength as we give in to it."

"Is that part of my first lesson?"

"In a way."

David grew thoughtful, looking at me in a quizzical manner. While we talked, I felt myself pulling away from him, from that place.

"I think, Paxton, we will continue this conversation later."

He had barely gotten the words out when a powerful force seemed to grab me and hurl me into a black place. I experienced a dizzying sensation as I fell. A great pressure kept me from screaming.

The next thing I knew, I hovered near the ceiling in a brightly lit room, feeling anxious without quite knowing why. Men and women in institution-green scrubs and masks practiced their urgent trade. I heard them talking about their patient.

"We're losing her!"

The room exploded with activity.

"Blood pressure's eighty over forty!"

A monitor showed the blips of a heart beat slowing.

"Give me one mil atropene, stat! I need a bolus of fluids and a Dopamine drip. Now! We need to raise her blood pressure."

A nurse inserted a needle into the patient's arm. Another produced a plastic bag of clear fluid.

The doctor spoke matter-of-factly. "She's in shock. Must be some internal blood loss. Get me four units, type O positive."

Another physician removed a pillow from under the patient's head. "Set up for intubation and get an Ambu bag on her," he commanded. He inserted a tube into the woman's mouth. In another minute, air was being pumped into her lungs.

I watched from my floating perch, wondering why I was there. Something seemed familiar, but I couldn't put my finger on it. The woman's face was covered with dirt and blood from a head wound and her features seemed distorted with facial swelling. A minute passed and then another while the crew of professionals worked their magic.

"Pressure's up to one-ten over sixty."

The blip increased to a steady pace.

"She's stabilizing, but we've got to get her to surgery and find out where she's losing blood. Call Parker and put him on alert."

I surveyed the scene for a few more minutes before I felt myself being drawn backwards. The room faded and I seemed to fly through dark space until, suddenly, I found myself sitting cross-legged at David's feet, stunned by my adventure.

"What on earth happened?" I asked, feeling dizzy and disoriented.

"Tell me what you experienced," David said.

I told him everything I had seen and heard. As I spoke, the truth gradually dawned.

"That was me on the table, wasn't it? I'm not dead."

"Goodness, no, you're as alive as I am."

"That's heartening," I said, unable to keep the sarcasm from my voice. "What triggered that little trip?"

"Apparently, your body didn't respond to treatment, and your presence was required in case you died. If you had, you wouldn't have been able to return here."

“Not return? But I love it here.” I heaved a giant sigh. "Nothing makes sense to me anymore. David, just exactly who are you, where am I, and why am I here?"

"As I explained, I am a teacher. You are simply where you have always been—in mind. You are nowhere and yet everywhere. You made a request, asked to be shown what to do. My job is to point you in the right direction."

"Which is?"

"In order to fulfill your purpose, the reason you were born, you also must become a teacher. I will provide you with the basic information you will need to do this. In the teaching, you will learn and grow yourself."

"I'm not a teacher, just a simple housewife! My education is sadly lacking. I couldn't teach a bunch of kids anything. I can't even control my own daughter."

"It is not a matter of control," David said, "and you won't be teaching in a classroom. Education is not required, only wisdom."

"That's a laugh. What makes you think I'm so all-fired wise?"

David's smile was gentle. "You may draw upon wisdom that is available to all who listen. Whenever others come to you for answers, listen to the voice within, and be willing to share your knowledge. By doing this, you will help many to live better."

I couldn't help it. Anger roiled up inside me and bubbled to the surface like a steaming cauldron of witch's brew. "Damn it, David! I don't want to be a teacher. I know so little myself, how could I tell anyone else how to live?"

"You'll be surprised at just how much you do know. In fact, all knowledge is available to you, if you will but ask to know it."

"You make absolutely no sense! Damn, but you make me angry. I don't want to hear any more of your crap. You want me to go out and tell people how to live? Well, when am *I* going to learn how?" I wanted to shake him. Instead, I stood and began to run, wanting to get as far away from David as I could. No more lessons. I just wanted to go home.

Or did I? I felt so content here most of the time. The place was alive with color and sensation. Everything seemed to reflect an inner peace. When David touched me, I felt nothing but love.

I stopped, thinking I should be out of breath. I wasn't. This place didn't allow for such things, I guessed.

Leaning against the broad, strong trunk of a glorious oak, I closed my eyes, trying to place myself back in my former world. I imagined looking up from a supine position as someone fitted a plastic mask over my mouth and nose. Excruciating pain shot through my body and I groaned. I forced my eyes open and the agony disappeared.

How could I possibly return to a world of such physical and emotional pain?

An old man and a young girl walked by, their heads nearly touching as they engaged in lively conversation. It seemed that everyone here had something to talk about.

I wondered how much time had passed since my accident. "Excuse me," I said, interrupting the girl in the middle of a sentence. "Can you tell me what time it is?"

The old man smiled. "It is the present moment, of course."

Hardly what I had expected.

"No, no. I mean what hour is it? I'm trying to figure out how long I've been here."

"Does it matter?" he asked.

"Well, I..." I paused, not sure of the answer.

"What is past, is past; what is in the future is yet to be. What is now must be nurtured and enjoyed. Glean the most from it." He smiled benevolently, and the couple continued on their way.

Another thing to think about tomorrow, I decided, feeling a bit like Scarlett O'Hara. So much information had been thrown my way. When would I have time to sift through it all?

Sighing, I retraced my steps. David sat cross-legged in the grass, staring out across the water. He must have seen me from the corner of his eye, because he turned and beckoned to me.

I sat next to him. "David, I'm sorry I let my anger get the best of me. Frankly, I'm not used to letting my emotions have free rein, but the thought of having to change my whole life feels, well, threatening."

"This is a safe place. Here, you may say anything you wish. Express your anger. Talk about your feelings. Ask what you will."

Gathering my thoughts, I said, "There's something I'm curious about. Last night, that man who passed us said 'David is an angel.' At the time, I thought he was telling me how he felt about you. Now, I'm wondering. Are you an angel? A real, honest-to-goodness one?"

David laughed and nodded. "A real, honest-to-goodness one, indeed."

So many questions flew through my mind, I didn't quite know where to start.

"Are you my guardian angel?"

"No. As I said, I am a teacher. You are but one of many students."

How disappointing. I had hoped I was special.

"You are special," he said, reading my thoughts again, "because you are my current student."

"And it is the present moment."

David appeared delighted. "Yes."

"You look so—human," I said, lost in the warm depth of his dark eyes. Despite my efforts, I couldn't help thinking of him with desire and blushed, knowing he probably sensed every emotion. A rush of love filled me.

"I'm embarrassed. Just a few short hours ago, I sat crying because my husband had been unfaithful. Now, I think I'm falling in love with you."

To my consternation, David laughed. "Of course you love me, and I love you. That is our natural state of being. But you are not *in* love with me." He touched my hand. "You have fallen for a vision, your idea of your perfect soul mate. If you could see me as I really am, you would not relate to me on this level. I am a being of light and, in reality, have no form at all except for what you have created to help you understand what I tell you. Do not be embarrassed by your feelings."

Somehow, this didn't make me feel better. I decided to change the subject.

"So... What is the first lesson?"

David smiled. "A much safer subject."

I shrugged.

"Very well, then, let us begin." He placed his fingertips together and stared in thought for a moment before he spoke.

"There is a single law governing all of life, though it has many names. Some people refer to it as a law of attraction. Others, more pessimistic, call it the law of retribution. Christians point to it when they quote their scriptures... *It is done unto you as you believe.* You might simply say it is cause and effect based on your belief system. I call it the Law of Life."

"Sort of like Karma?"

"What do you know about Karma?"

"Only what I've read or seen on television. It means, I think, that when we do something bad, we get punished for it or have to live through the same thing in another lifetime."

David laughed. "A rather simplified explanation. And what if someone does something good? Will he be rewarded?"

"I hadn't thought of it that way, but I guess so."

"Most people ignore that aspect, I'm afraid. The word carries with it a negative connotation."

"Then it can go either way? I mean, this law you're talking about can have both positive and negative results?"

David nodded, obviously pleased that I understood what he had said so far. "Every thought, word or deed is cause to a new effect. Depending on the nature of the cause, the effect can turn out wonderful or disastrous."

"You said every thought, word or deed. I can see how things I do, or even things I say, have an effect on my world, but thought? That's inconceivable."

“On the contrary. Last evening, you told me a story about how you wanted to leave a volunteer position, but did nothing about it. Yet, the Law of Life complied, and you were released from the job, even though you did nothing."

My mind felt taxed. Understanding came hard.

"Not the way I wanted it to happen, though."

"Precisely. If you take no action to follow your thought, the Law is left to figure things out for itself, so to speak. If you think back, however, you may have acted without realizing you were doing so. Perhaps you came in late a few times, spoke brusquely to a child, forgot to do a report, or adopted an attitude of 'I don't care if I'm here or not'."

David was being harsh with me. Somehow he knew.

"You just described everything I did. This doesn't seem quite fair. You seem to be aware of everything about me, and I know nothing about you."

"I understand little about how you experience living, Paxton, but I do know you. I know you're far better than you give yourself credit for. You're intelligent and kind and capable of a tremendous outpouring of empathy and love."

I wanted to cry. No one had ever spoken of me in such a wonderful way. Not since I was a little girl. Not since my mother cuddled me on her lap and told me how much she loved me and how important I was to her. When had I stopped thinking of myself as loveable or important?

"You *are* important, Paxton. In the next few days, you'll realize just how much you contribute to Life."

Suddenly, I wanted to hear more.

"All right, let's say it's true that the mere act of thinking can cause something to happen. How does it work?"

David looked pensive, apparently trying to decide how I'd understand best. He placed his finger tips together again, forming a sort of open-weave basket effect.

"The Law of Life is an intelligent force. It is behind everything that has ever happened, is happening now, or will occur in the future. It is impersonal and totally without judgment, providing whatever we demand without first asking whether or not it is good for us or bad. It is most generous, constantly giving. Because it is non-judgmental, we often end up experiencing things we'd rather not experience. This results from not knowing we have asked."

"David, I'd know if I asked for something."

"Are you quite sure?"

"Absolutely. And I'm also sure things have happened to me when I definitely didn't make any requests. Like my accident." I recalled my words on the beach. *Show me what to do. Whatever it takes, just give me a sign.* Somehow, I couldn't conceive that my accident had come from my cry for help. Especially since I had meant that help to put my marriage back together. "I certainly wouldn't ask to be flung off the edge of a mountain into a tree."

"Your need was immediate," David said. "What you learn here will indeed help you put your life back on track."

"But an accident, David!"

"The accident had nothing to do with your prayer. But the fact is, it happened. You asked for help. The Law of Life is opportunistic and took advantage of the situation to comply with your request.

"And what about the other car? Did those people deserve to be involved in my problem?"

"They had a belief system that made conditions fall into place. Their involvement actually had nothing to do with you, although each of you was a convenience to the others."

"Riddles again, David? Speak plainly. I want to understand."

David drew in a deep breath and let it out. "This is difficult. I want you to understand everything, but I know that you can only understand what you are ready to accept. I'll just tell you what I know to be true. It's up to you to accept or reject it."

"Choice."

"Exactly. The Law of Life works most precisely when what we think or say coincides with what is deep within us. Our patterns of belief prevail. If you say, today, I am a happily married woman, can you believe it?"

I snorted. "Of course not. I know Robert is involved with someone else. How can I be happy?"

"In this case, the Law of Life focuses on what you really believe because that is where your emotion is; that is where your power lies. It differentiates between what you say and what you think is true."

"Then it doesn't really have to be true. I have only to believe it is. But I believed I was happily married before. I didn't know I wasn't until Robert proved otherwise."

David gave me a questioning look.

"Okay, so I wasn't exactly happy."

Admitting this felt strange. I expected to be devastated; instead it seemed a burden had been lifted from my shoulders.

"David, do you think I wasn't really in love?"

"There are myriad ways to love in a thousand different degrees. People say they love tacos, or New York City, because these things strike a chord within them. Other than your family, what are some of the things you have said you love?"

"Gosh, probably a million things. Walking alone on a deserted beach. Sitting on a rock overlooking a mountain brook. Crisp apples freshly picked from a tree. Gardening. Travel. Spanky, a fox terrier I had when I was a child. My friend, Moira Plunkett."

Tears gathered in the corners of my eyes.

"All things that give you pleasure in some sense."

"Yes."

"As does your daughter."

"Absolutely."

"And Robert?"

I couldn't answer. How long had it been since I'd found pleasure in Robert's company? Far longer than I cared to admit. I liked being an important man's wife. But did I like being Robert's wife? I began to realize he had simply fulfilled my desire to be needed.

"I don't know," I finally said.

"Wonderful. Recognizing there is still something to discover about yourself is a beginning."

CHAPTER FIVE

THE LESSON CONTINUES

I HAD A vague sensation of time passing, but was never sure what time it might be. The sun seemed to stay directly overhead for hours. Often we sat in silence, mulling over what the other had said. I admit I did more *mulling* than David. Frequently when one of us spoke again, I couldn't be sure if ten minutes or an hour had gone by.

Sometimes other conversations intruded as people walked by and I'd find myself listening. *There are many roads to spiritual awareness. Some take longer than others. But know this, we are all on a pathway.* Then we'd be off on a tangent, discussing something new.

"If there are many paths to awareness," I mused, "how can I convince people the way you're teaching me is the *right* way to go?"

"Not everyone will believe you, Paxton. Don't even think that. But that doesn't mean they are wrong. Or right. Everything is a matter of perception, and their rejection means only that they cannot accept your words yet."

"Yet?" I asked. "What if they never do?"

"That," David said, "is not your problem. St. Thomas Aquinas once said, *We must love them both—those, whose opinions we share and those, whose opinions we reject. For both have labored in the search for truth and both have helped us in the finding of it."*

A few minutes passed before I spoke again.

"What is awareness, anyway?"

"What do you think it is?"

I struggled with my thoughts for a few minutes and finally said, "Wisdom, I suppose."

"And what is wisdom?"

"Good judgment."

David tried to draw me out. "Based on...?"

"Mmmm. Knowledge?"

"More than that."

I closed my eyes. Somehow, I felt I could *see* better this way. When I spoke, it seemed as though something within fed me the words. "A sense of knowing something that you could not understand through ordinary means. Clarity of thought."

David wriggled with excitement. "Now you're getting it. I knew you would."

"How do I gain wisdom?" I asked, wanting to explore the possibilities of what had just happened.

"By listening to your inner voice."

"Like Joan of Arc? I always wondered if she wasn't actually schizophrenic."

David laughed. "No, I don't mean voices. By inner voice, I mean intuition. What becomes obvious to you, consciously, is first made clear inwardly. That is what you just did a moment ago."

Sighing, I said, "I think that was a fluke. I can't remember too many times when I had this so-called thought clarity."

"That's because you rarely took the time to listen to your inner voice. Sometimes it takes a mental slap across the face to get you to notice."

"Like a cheating husband," I said. "Why is that?"

David did that basket weave thing with his fingers again. "Often when things are going good in your life, you forget to honor the spiritual part of you. Then, to become clear, your subconscious must first stir things up, which you certainly did just before you came here. You were confused, and confusion is like a layer of sand at the bottom of a jar full of water. If you let it stand undisturbed, eventually the water evaporates and what's left is sand. But if you pour new ideas into your mind, it's like pouring clear water into the jar. After a time, the sand is all gone and only clarity remains."

Our conversations continued. Somewhere at the back of my mind I was aware of a parallel existence. Machines droned and beeped. Men and women dressed in white or green turned me while they smoothed wrinkled sheets. Others poked me with needles. All treated me gently. I didn't actually seem to be there, but I was conscious of the dimly lit hospital room where I lay in a narrow bed. Alex sat, head bowed, holding my hand.

Robert's shadow covered her when he came through the door looking worried.

"Alex, honey," he said, startling her. "It's time to go home. You spend far too many hours here."

"I can't help it, Dad. I keep thinking I caused this. I wasn't very nice to Mom that morning. If I'd just...."

Robert couldn't hide his guilty look. "Don't ask me how I know, but her accident wasn't your fault."

"That's the whole point, Daddy. We don't know that it was an accident. What if she plunged down that hill on purpose? What if she tried to commit suicide?"

Oh, no, I thought. She can't believe that.

"Sweetheart, listen," Robert said, putting his arm around her shoulder. "Your mom and I talked about separating that day. If she meant to kill herself, I'm the one to blame, not you."

I could scarcely believe I'd heard him correctly. Had he just taken responsibility for something? In all the years we had been together, never once had he admitted fault. Never had he said, 'I'm sorry.' Was there hope for Robert after all? Hope for *us*?

"Separating?" Alex asked. "You mean like a divorce? Daddy, how could you?"

"Don't worry, honey. That discussion is over. I'm here for you and your mother now."

Did that mean he felt that he had made a mistake? Was his affair over? I wanted to hear more, but I knew he wouldn't tell Alex the gory details.

The scene faded. I felt torn between two worlds. In one, my daughter sat by my bed and read to me—poetry, the classics, things she knew I loved, even though she had always resisted reading them herself. In the other, I sat with a beautiful man taking in so much information, I wasn't sure I'd ever remember it all. Now, David watched me, interested in what I had been saying.

"Earlier, when I asked where I am, you said I'm where I've always been. In mind."

"Yes," he said.

I waited, knowing he'd continue eventually.

"Mind is where everything takes place."

"I'm afraid I don't understand. Are you saying that what's in my mind is what I experience?"

David smiled. "You tell me."

God, I hated when he did that. "How the heck am I supposed to know? Maybe... Maybe this whole thing is my imagination. Or perhaps it's a..." I searched for the right word. "...a miracle."

David's smile broadened. I sensed he was about to tell me something extraordinary.

"Miracles are naturally occurring events. You may think they happen without your input or influence, but that simply isn't true. You create the atmosphere for them to take place. The key to miracles is intent."

Another riddle, it seemed. I raised questioning eyebrows.

"Have you ever studied Greek mythology?" he asked.

"In high school," I admitted.

"Tell me the common thread that runs throughout these tales?"

He seemed to always be taxing my brain, but I finally came up with an answer.

"There's a problem to be solved."

"What else?"

"The hero leaves the safety and comfort of home to solve it."

"Go on."

"He spends years on a long journey and has many adventures along the way, solving smaller problems which in some way give him insight into the resolution of the reason he's on the journey. He often gets sidetracked from his original mission." I paused. "In a way, that sounds like my life, so far."

"Aha. And all that you have done has created the atmosphere that led you here. Do you consider that a miracle?"

"Not exactly." Now I sounded like him. "Are we back to cause and effect?"

"The Law of Life."

"So let me get this straight. Everything I ever did in my whole life led up to my being here with you. Or rather it put me on a road where I finally asked for a miracle and my asking was the cause of..." I gestured, indicating everything around me. "...this."

"Exactly."

I lay back, my arms behind my head, thinking about all that he had tried to teach me. So much information. So *little* information. It was nearly time for me to leave, David had told me. And we had barely tackled the first lesson. In the time that was left, would he be able to cover the rest?

"David, I want to understand as much as possible. Let me see if I can summarize what I've learned so far. Basically, the first lesson is this: There is a creative law of life that we can use, and we have choice as to how we use it."

"Correct."

"Good. When do we start the second lesson?"

He smiled, enigmatically. "Another time, perhaps."

"Have I learned all I need to know?"

"Oh, no, Paxton. There is so much more."

I felt myself turning red. "Which you aren't about to tell me, right? If there is no time but the present, why don't you just speak up and tell me everything now?"

David looked at me, one eyebrow raised. "You will know what you need to know. Simply turn within and ask."

I sulked. "Maybe I won't go back."

"Ah, but you have to go. You must reveal all that I have told you to the world."

"I have to? That's contradictory. You said I have choice."

"Yes."

He had me. He knew I would return. So did I.

"Why me?"

"Why not you?"

I shook my head. His way of answering questions with questions simply to make me think infuriated me.

"I'm just a nobody. No one will listen to me. You need a Mahatma Ghandi, not a Paxton Michaels."

"There were those who refused to listen to Ghandi as well. No great teacher has found accord in every student. It is perfectly acceptable for people to choose to listen or not. If they don't, it is not your concern. You are simply meant to speak the truth, for truth accepted will heal the world."

"And just how am I to disseminate all this information—that I don't necessarily have, by the way?"

"That is entirely up to you."

I couldn't believe I'd heard him correctly. I raged at David. "You aren't being fair! You've practically charged me with healing the world, but you'll leave me on my own to find out how to do it?"

Smiling his gentle smile, David grasped my shoulders and held my gaze. "Each of us has a part in healing. We are born into the world naked, with no concept of how we are going to accomplish what we have set out to do. We choose the task and then find our way."

"I didn't really choose this task," I grumbled.

"Ah, but you did. Long before your mother cradled you in her arms, you knew your purpose. You have simply forgotten it until now. Perhaps it will help to know you are not alone. Others have preceded you. Some will join you. Still others will follow. And I will be with you when you need me. When you ask for an answer, it is my voice you will hear."

I wanted to believe him, but I had my doubts and said so.

"Doubts are good," David said, nodding vigorously. "It helps one keep an open mind. When the mind is open, something always comes along to fill it up."

"Or close it."

"That, too, of course. The choice..."

"Yeah, I know... is mine."

He nodded and sighed. "The time for you to return to your physical world is drawing near."

I knew he was right; I could feel the pull of my other existence. Yet I had so many questions. It didn't seem possible he could turn me loose with such a small amount of information. I had mere hours of instruction. I needed days, weeks. Maybe years.

"Come," said David. "We'll walk."

I followed him out of the shadows where we had been sitting into the sunshine. Butterflies danced among the flowers, and birds serenaded us with their songs.

"It's so beautiful here," I said once again.

David looked thoughtful. "Beauty, too, is a matter of perception." He turned to me. "I shall miss you, Paxton Michaels."

Not nearly as much as I'll miss you, I thought, forgetting momentarily that he would know what I was thinking. I wanted to cry out, 'You're the love I've always wanted.' Instead, I said, "I hope I'm up to this."

David patted my hand. "Remember, each of us has choice over what to accept or reject of what is revealed, just as we have choice over our experiences. You'll encounter resistance from those who choose to remain as they are."

"It isn't going to be easy, is it?"

"Not exactly."

He smiled one last time. "The machines at your bedside indicate an increase in brain activity. They know you're coming."

CHAPTER SIX

THE RETURN JOURNEY

"MOM, MOM. WAKE UP."

I heard Alex's voice and felt a tug at my waist. Suddenly, I was free falling, zooming back through the tunnel. In a flash, I slammed with a well-defined jolt into the physical world and opened my eyes. I groaned, for this world was filled with horrendous pain. My head pounded. My right leg felt like someone had dropped an anvil on it. My rib cage throbbed. I was in agony.

"Alex," I said. My voice sounded weak, but there was no way I could make it come out stronger. I lifted my hand to touch her cheek. Her worried face had never seemed so beautiful. I felt a rush of love that threatened to spill over into tears. How, even for an instant, could I not have wanted to come back to her? Loving her was worth any pain I might have to endure.

"You cut your hair," I said. "When?"

"Days ago."

"No, when I left here yesterday, it was down to your waist."

Alex looked puzzled. "Yesterday? You've been in a coma almost three weeks."

There is no time but the present, I remembered, wondering how I could lose three weeks. That meant I had missed Alex's graduation.

A nurse rushed in and began taking my vital signs. Her tone was gentle, soothing. "There, there, dearie. You've been away for a long time. Just lie back and rest. Everything's gonna be all right."

"What..." My voice sounded harsh and grating. I cleared my throat and tried again. "What's wrong with me? How bad is it?"

The nurse patted my hand. "The doctor'll be in later to talk to you. He'll tell you everything."

"If you won't tell me yourself, it must be something awful."

"No, no," she assured me. "Now that you're back among the living, you'll be just fine."

My eyes pleaded.

Alex butted in. "You have a broken leg, Mommy."

She hadn't called me that in years.

"And you had some internal bleeding. They had to cut you open to find out where. A broken rib punctured your left lung, but they said you're okay now. It's your head injury we've all been worried about. A skull fracture, the doctor said." She began crying. "Oh, Mom, I thought you were going to die."

Her sobs drowned out the noise of the machines by my bed. Tubes and wires crisscrossed my body and hooked me to them.

"Don't cry, baby. I'm okay. Honest. In fact, I had a fantastic experience."

Alex looked at me, disbelieving. "What kind of experience?"

"I met an angel. He's the one who told me I had to come back."

Alex sobbed again. "They said you might not be right in the head when you woke up. If you woke up."

"I'm righter than I've ever been, darling. Now quit crying. You're getting me all wet."

The nurse busied herself taking my blood pressure again. "It's time for you to leave anyway, honey. Before you go home, better call your dad and let him know the good news."

Robert. I could hardly wait to see him.

Alex kissed my lips, something she hadn't done since she was six years old. "I'll be back later, Mom. I love you."

"Love you, too, hon."

I watched her go, grateful that, with her leaving, I could succumb to the self-pity that overwhelmed me. My body was a torture chamber that I'd have to call home until my bones and tissues healed. I tried to divert my thoughts by counting all the things about Alex that made me feel proud. She really was a good kid. With a shock, I remembered the thoughts I'd harbored before my accident. I constantly saw her faults, not her good points. David would have asked, *Did you fail to see her good points because she had faults? Or did she acquire faults because you failed to see her good points?*

The nurse returned with a syringe. "I know you just woke up, but your machines are tellin' me you're a bit agitated. Doctor Hunter left word to give you a sedative."

Hunter? I didn't know any Doctor Hunter. Must be some specialist Robert hired.

"My name's Sarah," the woman in white said. "I know you're hurting, but you'll be fine." She rolled me over gently and poked my butt with the needle. "I suppose I shouldn't be telling you this. Couple of days from now, we'll be transferring you, and you'll get some good help at Rancho."

"Rancho?"

"Rancho Los Amigos. One of the best rehab hospitals around."

I smiled. More evidence that Robert was taking care of me. I almost didn't want to remember what had happened with David. I wanted to go back to the way it used to be, with Robert making decisions, and with God safely off in the clouds where he didn't have to bother with my little, insignificant life. My last thought before drifting off to sleep was that the only thing I hoped I'd get to keep was Alex's new attitude.

Later, through a fog of medication, I heard Robert's voice talking to the doctor. "Let's get her out of here as soon as possible."

"We have a perfectly good therapy program here," the doctor replied. "And she'd be closer to home so you can visit easily."

"I've made up my mind. She belongs at Rancho."

The next few days were pain-filled. Now that I was awake, physical therapy started in earnest. As soon as Dr. Hunter—who, by the way, only came to see me once that I recall—gave the word, I was stuffed into an ambulance and carted off to Rancho Los Amigos Medical Center. There, I met Herman, an African American whose smile was radiant as a sunny day. He took his role as physical therapist seriously and didn't intend to let even one of my muscles atrophy. The rigors and stress of what he put me through made me wonder if he hadn't been trained in torture, rather than healing. Sometimes I screamed at him during a painful session, calling him terrible names, threatening to end his life if I ever got off my crutches. He never stopped encouraging me, and he never quit smiling.

Alex came to see me as often as she could. Robert's promise of a new car hadn't materialized, although he had purchased a ten year old Honda Accord for her to use. Rancho is located miles from Pacific Palisades, and it scared me to know she had passed her driver's test only weeks before. Because of recent changes in the law, she had to bring someone over twenty-five with her, and usually it was the hapless housekeeper that Robert had hired. Nevertheless, Alex's presence made the pressure of getting well more bearable.

"Where's your dad today?" I asked one Friday about a week after I had reawakened to the physical world. I had only seen him twice since the accident. Once when he came in to sign some papers, and again on the day I transferred hospitals. He always sent word with Alex that he hoped things were going well, but that he was tied up with a big account that consumed most of his waking hours.

"He's at the golf course, I guess." My raised eyebrows prompted her to defend him. "Honest, Mom, he works really hard most of the time."

I patted her hand. "I'm not saying he doesn't, baby. I just hoped he'd come see me since it's the weekend."

"I hardly ever see him, either. Thank goodness, he hired a housekeeper. At least I get a hot dinner." She smiled. "Mrs. Washington thinks I'm too skinny. She's trying to fatten me up."

"Not a bad idea," I said, eyeing her slender frame. "Has she been able to get anything green into you?"

"You mean like vegetables? Yeah, she makes an awesome brussel sprouts casserole with Parmesan cheese and artichoke hearts and bread crumbs."

"Brussel sprouts? Wow, your taste buds must have matured a lot while I was away."

Alex grinned. "And she has this great looking son, Brian, who picks her up at six every night. He's a basketball player at UCLA."

"Too old."

"Mom! He's only nineteen."

"And you're only sixteen and just out of high school. Nineteen year old men go to jail for dating adolescents."

"Only if something happens."

Frustrated, I shook my finger at her. "You're not dating a college man, young lady."

She huffed. "Dad already said I could."

"Well, we'll see about that."

The rest of our visit didn't go too well. When Herman came in with a chair to wheel me to therapy, Alex left. But not before she reminded me she had turned seventeen and that I'd missed her birthday.

"Herman," I said, "do you have any kids?"

"Sure do. A boy who's thirty. He's Sam. And a seven-year-old girl."

"Thirty and seven? How'd you manage that?"

"My girl was a change of life baby. But me and my wife are sure blessed by that child."

"What's her name?"

"Tina. Guess you can tell who I named her after."

"Tina Turner?"

"Yeah, her mama liked Moesha, but I won out. Course, Moesha's her middle name."

Herman pushed a button on the wall and double doors slammed open for us. He wheeled me to the edge of the whirlpool spa and gently lowered me into it. He never strayed far when I was in the churning pool. I think he worried that I might drown. I was finally out of my cast, and the swirling water soothed me.

Herman leaned against a wall, crossed one ankle over the other and settled down to wait.

"I guess boys are different from girls, but did you have any problem with Sam when he was a teenager?" I asked.

"Problem's too mild a word for it. He dropped out of high school, joined a gang, sold drugs, got a girl pregnant. You name it, he did it. But you know what? When he got to be twenty, he turned completely around. Married the girl who's the mama of his little boy. Got a job and went to night school. Now, he's got a bachelor's degree in economics and is working on his masters. If you're gonna ask me what happened, don't. I have no idea. He did it all himself."

"He simply chose a new direction. That's what life is all about. Making decisions to go a different way." I couldn't believe I'd just said that. The words that came out of my mouth didn't feel like mine, and most certainly wouldn't have been a few short weeks ago.

Herman nodded. "Yep, I guess you can say that. It sure seemed like that with Sam."

The room was quiet except for the bubbling water that washed my battered body with healing warmth. Neither of us said a word for a while. When I finally spoke, it was with a great longing to fold Alex into my arms and tell her how much I love her.

"Well, my daughter hasn't done all the things Sam did, but she still drives me crazy. Somehow, though, I think she'll turn out just fine."

When Herman had squeezed the last little bit of strength from my body with his demand for just one more leg lift, he took me back to my room.

"I hate you, Herman," I said as the man helped me back into bed. My body protested every movement.

"I know, pretty lady, but you're gonna love me in the end."

I shook my head. "Which can't come too soon."

Exercise always increases my normally voracious appetite. That evening, as I gobbled down my dinner while watching the Channel Seven news, a familiar voice surprised me.

"Hey, honey bunch. Got time for an old friend?"

"Moira!" I cried. She'd been faithful, coming to see me every day before I moved to Rancho, but her busy schedule didn't make it easy for her to trek east to Downey on a regular basis. I had missed her cheery face.

She gave me a fierce hug and jumped back when I grunted.

"Did I hurt you?"

"It's just these damned broken ribs. They're pretty much healed, but they still hurt."

Moira looked chastened. "I'm sorry. I'm used to your being healthy. Here, maybe this'll help."

She handed me a five-pound box of Heggy's chocolates. I looked up, astonished. "Have you been to Ohio?"

"No, I called and ordered them for you. Nothing better, hm?"

She was right. Chocolate always seemed to soothe whatever ailed me. I'd weigh two hundred pounds if I let myself succumb to my craving for the stuff. I opened the box, picked out a caramel and popped it into my mouth. "Want some?" The question came out garbled. Moira laughed and took a peanut cluster. We chewed, comfortable with being together again.

"I'm glad to see you looking a bit more normal," Moira said. "Last time, you were still groaning every time you lifted your hand an inch or two. And, honey, I have to tell you, I thought you were on your way out. Either that or you'd lost your mind."

"What do you mean?"

"Well, you kept talking about seeing angels."

I looked down at the candy on my lap, pretending to concentrate on picking out another delectable bit. I could feel her scrutinizing my response. Finally, I met her eyes. "I did see an angel. His name is David."

I sensed Moira backing away from the terror that I had somehow gone off the deep end.

"Don't close me out," I begged. "At least listen to what happened before you judge me too harshly."

She took a deep breath and blew it out between pursed lips while she examined the ceiling. Then, her decision made, she nodded. "I'll listen, honey. You've always been a sensible person. Whatever happened to you must have a reasonable explanation, and we'll find it together."

I doubted that she'd find my tale reasonable, but I had to tell someone. Alex always had something urgent to do the moment I mentioned my time away. The thought of telling Robert scared me. If he decided to leave me after all, he might use it against me. I imagined him getting up in court and the words he'd throw out to the judge. "Incompetent. Hears voices. Unfit mother." I wouldn't have a chance in hell to gain custody of Alex, even for the short time before she turned eighteen.

Grateful for Moira's friendship, I turned off the television, pushed my dinner tray aside, and told her the whole story. She listened intently, asked dozens of questions, never took her eyes from mine. When I had finished, she leaned back in her chair and crossed her arms, staring out the window. I waited for her response, nervous as a long tailed cat in a room full of rocking chairs. I sensed the moment she made her decision. She uncrossed her arms and smiled.

"Odd as it sounds, honey bunch, I believe you. Every damned word."

I was stunned and filled with gratitude. "You do? You're not just saying that? No one else believes me." I frowned. "You're not trying to humor me, are you?"

Moira reached over and gave my hand a pat. "I won't lie, Paxton. That's probably the wildest, most far-fetched story I've ever heard. But you are the sanest, most honest person I've ever met. If you say that's what happened, then that's what happened. Now, what are we going to do about it?"

"I don't know. I'm not even sure I want to do anything. David said I had to figure out how to tell people what he said. I have no idea how to go about it. Besides, if there's even half a chance that Robert and I can make our marriage work..."

Moira shook her head and looked away.

"What's the matter?" I asked. She shook her head again. "Moira! If there's something I need to know, tell me. Don't leave me in the dark like this."

"Paxton, I'm sorry. I'd give anything not to be the one to say this." She clasped her hands on her lap and examined them as though they were the most interesting things she had ever seen. "Robert is openly escorting that slut around town. I saw them at Spago's the other day, sitting in a booth, all kissy-huggy. When he looked up and saw me, he just raised his eyebrows and waved."

My spirits sank to an all-time low. I'd been harboring hope for our future and, suddenly, my prospects for happiness looked bleak.

CHAPTER SEVEN

CONFRONTING THE ENEMY

I PUT THE finishing touches on my makeup and combed my hair. When Robert came, he wouldn't find me looking sorry for myself. I'd let him talk and then pounce on him with my newly acquired knowledge.

His secretary had called earlier that day, letting me know that my husband would arrive at four o'clock. I wondered aloud how he'd managed to squeeze me onto his appointment calendar, but my sarcasm didn't faze his unflappable assistant. She simply confirmed that he had some papers for me to sign.

When he arrived, Robert was all business. No *Hi, how are you* or *I hope you're feeling better.* He walked in, sat down and opened his briefcase.

"I've been in touch with the insurance company. They've offered a settlement of $100,000, but that won't even put a dent in your medical bills. I've instituted a suit against the insurance firm and the driver of the car, as well as his father. He owns the vehicle. We're asking for complete coverage of your expenses, replacement of the car, and five million in damages. The father is CEO of a computer firm. He can afford it."

"Excuse me? You did this without consulting the injured party? Don't I have a say in the matter?"

"What could you possibly say? We might as well get some compensation from this. What easier way is there to put a couple of million in the bank?"

My mouth dropped open, and I stared at this man who had fathered my only child. "You think this is easy? Struggling day after day while my physical therapist grinds the last ounce of strength out of my torn and tattered body? This is the hardest thing I've ever done."

Robert grimaced. "Well, I didn't mean *you* had it easy. But this is, as the saying goes, an open and shut case."

David's words rang in my head. I had to take responsibility for what happened to me in life. If I'd paid more attention to road conditions, I'd probably have avoided the accident completely. The other car might have skidded and then righted itself and gone on. "It wasn't entirely his fault. If I hadn't been driving so fast, I wouldn't have been at that curve in the road, and the accident would never have happened."

I cringed under Robert's gaze. "That's rather ludicrous, don't you think? Your deductive reasoning skills are sadly lacking, Paxton. The boy skidded over the line into your lane. He's totally at fault. He as much as admitted it."

"Then he doesn't know I was speeding."

"And he never will. Your skid marks weren't long enough to measure since you went off the cliff. No one needs to know."

"That's dishonest, Robert. I won't sign those papers."

"You're being stupid."

"Perhaps. But it feels like I'm doing the right thing. Ask for payment of my medical bills if you want, but no damages."

Robert argued with me for another twenty minutes before angrily stuffing the papers back into his case. Then he pulled out another folder and handed it to me.

"What's this?" I asked.

"A notice that I've filed for divorce, for one thing. Our property settlement, for another. I'm being very fair. I'll pay you two thousand a month until Alex turns eighteen. You can have custody, of course. And you can stay in the house until it sells. I'll give you half the proceeds of the sale. Incidentally, there's a listing agreement that needs your signature in there, as well."

He unscrewed the top of his Montblanc pen and handed it to me, expecting acquiescence. Stunned, I simply stared. He shook the pen at me, as if calling my attention to it. All my good intentions about letting him talk and keeping my cool went out the window.

"You son-of-a-bitch. You told Alex you weren't thinking about divorce any more and that you'd be here for the two of us."

His tone sounded exasperated. "Look, Paxton, let's not kid ourselves. Our marriage is over. Besides, I only told her the *discussion* was over. It was. I had already made up my mind. And I am here for the two of you. You're being well taken care of, and I've hired a housekeeper to make sure Alex is, too." He paused and gave me a searching look. "How did you know I told her that?"

Remembering that I'd been in a coma during that conversation, at least as far as he was concerned, I hedged. "Alex told me," I fibbed before confronting him again. "So it's true that you're taking your little tramp out in public and showing her off to the world."

"That must be Moira talking."

"At least I have one friend who tells me the truth."

"I won't deny it, Paxton." He held out the pen again. "You might as well get this over with."

Furious, I knocked his precious Montblanc out of his hand. It flew across the room, and he scurried to retrieve it.

"You know, it might be wise if I read these before I sign."

Robert sighed. "Of course." He sat back in his chair and waited.

Sarcasm practically dripped down my chin when I spoke. "And, considering your legal acumen, I'm sure you'll agree that my attorney should take a look at these."

This surprised the heck out of him. "Your attorney? You don't need an attorney. That will just cost you a bundle of money. I'll take care of everything. It'll be cheaper."

So our marriage had come down to this. Dollars and cents. Letting Robert's lawyer handle both sides of our divorce would certainly be less expensive for him. He'd not only save attorney fees, but he'd make sure he got the bulk of our estate. I didn't even know how much money we had in savings, let alone what kind of stock we owned or how much the house was worth.

"Nevertheless," I said, "I'll let Jay Plunkett take a look at these before I sign."

"Jay Plunkett? Moira's husband? He's a probate attorney. Knows nothing about family law."

"That could be to your advantage. So why should you object?"

When Robert finally left, stomping out of the room like an angry little boy who hadn't gotten his way, the only thing I felt was relief. My muscles ached from the tension I'd been holding in them and, for the first time, I thought I might look forward to working with Herman the next day. My heart ached, too—for my failed marriage, for the loss of love, for Alex. She would be the one who suffered the most. Robert, evidently, was leaving it up to me to tell her the news.

"Oh, David," I whispered. "Where's all that wisdom you tried to impart now? What shall I do? What should I say to her?"

I listened, but the room was silent.

The next morning, a plump woman dressed in a brown gabardine skirt and wrinkled, white cotton blouse bustled in with a clipboard in her hand. She sat down beside my bed and introduced herself.

"I'm Mrs. Madsen. I hope you don't mind answering a few questions."

It was obvious from her brusque, business-like manner that she intended to ask them whether I minded or not.

"I understand your husband has filed for divorce," she said, consulting the paper attached to her clipboard. "And that he has published a notice of non-responsibility. He dropped a copy off to our accounting department yesterday afternoon."

"Non-responsibility? What does that mean?"

"It means that you will have to be responsible for your own hospital bills."

"That shouldn't be anything to worry about," I said, searching my mind for possible problems. "Our auto insurance carrier is working with the insurance company covering the driver of the car that hit me to take care of things. I'm also covered by my husband's health insurance."

"We've been told the other driver carried only the minimum coverage on his car."

"I thought the car belonged to the driver's father."

Mrs. Madsen consulted her notes. "Our sources say that the car was signed over to the son the day before the accident, on his eighteenth birthday, and the insurance was changed that day, as well."

I laughed, thinking how Robert prided himself on getting his facts straight. The kid's dad was pretty smart, putting his son on title as soon as he reached adulthood.

"This isn't a laughing matter, Mrs. Michaels. It's quite serious, as a matter of fact."

I stifled another giggle and nodded. "I'm sure it is. Please go on."

"Well..." She looked me in the eye for the first time since she had walked into the room. "Someone has to pay your bills. The insurance company will pay a portion of it, of course. And we can bill your husband's health insurer, but it's possible they'll refuse to pay. Do you have a job?"

"No."

"Will you be receiving spousal support?"

"My husband will undoubtedly fight me tooth and nail to avoid that."

"Do you own any property?"

"Robert and I have a home in Pacific Palisades. Frankly, I don't know if we own any other property. Robert takes care of all our investments."

I noticed she wrote down everything I said. "Why do you want to know that?" I asked.

"We'll want you to sign a promissory note for the balance of your care. Even if you don't, the County can file a lien against your properties."

I must have had panic written on my face because she explained, "The County rarely forecloses on a lien, but when you sell your house, they'll want their money." She looked down, and then up at me again. "Plus interest."

"So how far in debt am I?"

"Prior to any payment from your insurance..." She consulted her papers again. "Just under three hundred thousand dollars."

This time, I laughed so hard, my not-quite-healed ribs hurt. "That's really funny," I told her. "My husband must be getting a real charge out of this. How fast can the County put a lien on our house?"

Mrs. Madsen looked confused. "Why, I don't know."

"Then you'd better go get the ball rolling, Mrs. M." I continued to laugh.

She gathered up her clipboard and backed out of the room. "I'm sure I'll be back, Mrs. Michaels."

After she had gone, I dialed Jay Plunkett's office. His secretary put me through as soon as I told her my name.

"Paxton!" he said. "How the hell are you?"

"Aside from a few aching but mending bones and a tendency to list when I walk, I'm just great. There is one little problem, though."

His tone sobered. "What's that?"

"Robert served me with divorce papers last night, and he filed a notice of non-responsibility. If my senses haven't taken leave, I think he's trying to make sure I get as little as possible from our assets. I need your help."

"I'm not a divorce attorney, but I can help you find a really good one."

"I want you, Jay. I trust you."

"It will be to your benefit if another..."

"Forget it. No one else. You. I need you, my friend. Especially since you never liked Robert very much, anyhow."

Jay chuckled. "Was it that obvious?"

"Oh, you tried. Moira, too. Both of you were nice to him, and he tolerated you, but if it hadn't been for me, you would never have been his friend."

"Look," he said. "I'll read over your papers and sic someone on finding out just what Robert has banked for his future. Maybe we can get another attorney to do this with me to make sure I don't goof up. How could I say no to you?"

"There's one more problem."

"Which is?"

"I don't think I have any money for a retainer."

"Robert kept a tight rein on the finances, I take it."

"Something like that," I admitted.

He was silent for a moment. I wasn't sure whether he was considering not taking the case without a retainer, or if he was angry that I hadn't taken more responsibility for my life up until now. Actually, I was pretty angry about that, myself.

Finally, he spoke. "Let's not worry about money for now. I'll take care of everything."

When I hung up the phone, the enormity of what was happening hit me. Herman found me sobbing when he came in to take me to therapy.

That evening, when the night crew had turned down the lights and I was supposed to be sleeping, I called out David's name.

"Where are you? You said you'd be here when I needed you."

"I'm here, Paxton."

My already red eyes teared again as I felt his love. "Did you know Robert never gave up his intent to leave me?"

"I suspected as much."

"Couldn't you have told me?"

David answered with a question. *"What if he had changed his mind?"*

I knew what he meant. If I had a pre-conceived notion that Robert wasn't going to stick around, I wouldn't have believed him if he said he would stay.

"Things will never be the same, David."

"There is never a status quo, my friend," he said. *"The only thing you can be sure of is that things will change."*

"What will I do? What *must* I do in order to grow into the person you want me to be?"

"The woman I want you to be is the one you want to be. What are you willing to become? Your world cannot change if you stay the same. What world are you willing to create?"

I sighed. Being an enlightened woman takes a lot of work, I decided. "Okay, I'm asking again. What must I do?"

"Look within, Paxton Michaels. Your soul knows the answer."

CHAPTER EIGHT

GOING HOME

"WELL, YOUNG LADY," my doctor said, "it's been a long road, and that staph infection kept you here longer than you deserved." He consulted his chart. "Let's see, we've solved most of the neurological problems, and your sense of balance is coming back." He smiled. "I think you can go home tomorrow."

"Home," I said. A few weeks ago, *home* meant security, motherhood, a husband who, I presumed, loved me. What a different connotation the word had today. When I thought about it, home had also meant compulsive cleaning, arguments, frustration, and despair. This morning, home simply meant a place to stay until I decided where I wanted to go next; a place where I could try to make peace with my daughter and myself.

Dr. Rodriguez scribbled something on a pad of paper. "I'll arm you with a prescription for pain, since you're not completely healed yet, and you'll have to come in three times a week for therapy for a while." He handed me the prescription, smiled, and patted my hand. "You've been a good patient, Mrs. Michaels. Not many people work as hard as you have to get well."

I laughed. "I can't take credit for the hard work, Doctor. Herman pushes me, sometimes to the point where I'd like to throw him off a cliff. If it wasn't for him, I'd be nowhere near ready to go home."

"Can you arrange for someone to take you home tomorrow?"

I assured him I could. When he left, I called Moira. She agreed to pick me up and the following morning was in my room packing my stuff.

"I think you're as anxious to get me out of here as I am to go," I said, laughing.

"You got that right, honey bunch. I hate this ride down here. Busy freeways always bug me, and this is one of the busiest as far as I can see."

I frowned, just on the verge of asking her to chauffer me back and forth to the hospital for therapy. Maybe I'd have to depend on Alex.

As if she'd read my mind, Moira continued. "Of course, I'd do anything for you. The doc told me on the way in that you had to come back for some more muscle crunching or whatever it is that handsome African-American does to you." She cocked her head, closed one eye and stared at the ceiling. "Think Jay would mind if I took a lover?"

I laughed, knowing Moira would never consider having an affair. Her fantasy world, however, was a topic for conversation. Even Jay enjoyed the fruits of her imagination, and they played little games to stimulate it further. Suddenly, depression hit me like a rock. Robert had deplored anything imaginative about our sex life. One position, ten minutes max, over and done with. I was on the verge of tears the entire trip home. When we turned the corner and the house loomed into view, fear surged through my body. I didn't know what to expect when I walked through the door.

Moira helped me out of the car and handed me my crutches. Where I had always welcomed coming home before, the house now seemed alien and forbidding to me. Everything seemed in perfect order. Symmetrical flower beds, neatly trimmed shrubs, perfectly edged lawn. Nothing out of place, nothing to suggest that anyone but the gardener cared. I remembered how, when Alex was a toddler, Robert crabbed if she left a toy in the yard or her tricycle in the driveway, because it destroyed the ambiance.

"You look like a tourist seeing this place for the first time," Moira said.

"I *feel* like I'm seeing it for the first time. It's beautiful, but cold. Sterile, almost."

My friend carried my luggage and the paraphernalia I had collected in my weeks away. I hobbled to the door and opened it just as a silver Cadillac pulled into the driveway behind Moira's car. A woman hopped out and waved.

"Yoo hoo, excuse me," she said. "Who are you?"

I waited while she clicked her three-inch heels up the sidewalk to join us.

"I'm Paxton Michaels. Who are you?"

"Rita Dunn from Dunn Properties," she said, handing me a card with her colored photo on it, obviously a glamour shot. It looked nothing like her. "You can't go in there this morning. I'm holding a broker's open house from ten to one."

I gave her an astonished look. "Today? No one told me."

Her face took on a sympathetic expression, but she was adamant. "I'm sorry. Mr. Michaels made it clear that we needed to do this as soon as possible. You'll have to go somewhere else until about one-thirty or so."

"She doesn't *have* to do anything, Ms. Dunn," Moira said. "Mrs. Michaels just got out of the hospital, and she needs to rest."

"It's totally inappropriate for an owner to be home during a broker's open house," Rita said. "I need complete freedom to speak with the other brokers about their opinions of the house, and they need to be totally free to say what they really think. An owner wandering around inhibits them."

"Like I really care," I told her, but caved in anyway. "Moira, may I come to your place until it's time to go see Jay?" I had made an appointment to meet him that afternoon.

"Of course, you can, doll. But why? This is your house. You have some say in what's going on."

I had decided that I wanted out of Robert's house as quickly as possible and into my own place, even if it was a simple, one-bedroom apartment. The quicker the thing sold, the faster I could get on with my life. *And your mission*, something prompted me.

I shook my head at Moira. "No, it's okay. Just put my stuff in the bedroom closet. I'll wait here."

Rita smiled, triumphantly, and clicked back to her car to remove an open house sign and a bouquet of balloons from her trunk. She pounded the sign into the lawn and tied the helium-filled balloons to the stake. "Helps call attention to us," she called in explanation.

She opened the rear car door and brought out a huge platter of sandwiches. She put it on top of the car and pulled a case of sparkling cider out, as well. "Have to feed the multitudes to get them to come," she said, laughing, "even to a great house like this." She carried the cider to the door, then went back for the food. "I'll let you ladies out of the driveway in just a minute."

She and Moira exited the house at the same time, and I soon found myself back my friend's Lexus, on our way to the Plunkett residence.

After a morning of talk and lunch on the patio, I felt like I'd been on a twenty mile trek. "God, I'm tired. What I wouldn't do for a nap."

"Do you want to postpone your appointment with Jay?"

Yes! my body screamed. My brain responded differently. "No, let's get it over with."

At two on the dot, Jay's secretary ushered us into his office.

"Paxton, this is Irene Turner. She's one of the best family law attorneys around, and specializes in subduing husbands who cheat on their wives."

I shook hands with a woman who epitomized the term 'an imposing figure'. She stood about five-feet-nine, and must have weighed a solid two-hundred pounds. Her graying blonde hair was pulled back in a French twist, and she wore a power suit of navy blue wool, obviously quality, obviously pricey. She got right down to business.

"Robert Michaels might have a brilliant attorney, but in this case, he didn't do his homework. Your husband apparently thought you'd just roll over, pick up your pen, and sign your life away. Until one of you moves out of the house—and my sources have it that neither of you has done so—his income is still considered community property. Besides, Paxton, no judge in his right mind would let him get away with what he's trying to do. We have to get him in front of that judge."

"I don't want to take more than my fair share," I said, appalled at how timid I sounded.

"You're entitled to half. Half his money, half your properties, half of your investments, part of his pension. Shall I go on?"

"I didn't contribute half."

Irene sighed and threw the papers she'd been holding onto the desk. "Why is it that women either want everything or nothing?"

I frowned. "What do you mean?"

"Some wives, believing they've been screwed by their husbands, want to turn him into a pitiful remnant of what he was when they married and send him to the poor house. Others figure it's their fault that the bastard is running around on them. While they feel guilty, they let the guy talk them into taking little or nothing from the marriage, no matter how long they've been together. They ignore the fact that the jerk wouldn't let them work or kept them barefoot and pregnant. In that case, it's the woman who ends up at the lower end of the stick."

"I take it that you equate me with the latter."

"Correct."

Jay interrupted. "If you think you didn't contribute to Robert getting to where he is today, think again. Who made ends meet when he was first starting out? Who entertained all his scuzzy friends and clients? Who maintained the house he bought so he could show off how well he's doing? Who helped him build the image that he was bright and successful?"

I laughed. "You make me sound like a saint."

Jay smiled, too. "All I'm saying is that I don't want him to take you to the cleaners."

"I know. I'll look at everything again and let you know what I'm going to do." I reached out and took his hand. "I really appreciate your taking this on for me." I included Irene in my gratitude. "Both of you."

"You're worth it, my friend," Jay said. "Besides, if I didn't, Moira would divorce me; and I definitely put her into the category of those who would take everything they can get."

I knew he didn't mean that. Every time he looks at his wife, his eyes glaze over and his expression goes all soft, the same way my cat looks when I scratch her rear end. Despite having been married for nearly twenty years, Moira and Jay love each other as much, if not more, than they did when they were newlyweds. How I envied them.

When I finally got home, Rita Dunn had gone. Evidence of her open house remained behind in the trash compactor. I sat in the sunroom and read every word of every document Irene had provided. What amazed me most was how wealthy Robert had become over the years. A title search had turned up three apartments, twenty-four units in all, and a beach house in Malibu that I knew nothing about. Jay had pointed out that there were quitclaim deeds to Robert that purported to carry my signature. These apparently allowed him to hold title as his sole and separate property. It seemed that he'd anticipated our divorce for years and went so far as forgery to make sure I got very little.

Robert owned a healthy stock portfolio, had an individual checking account with more than a hundred-thousand in it, and certificates of deposit totaling almost three-quarters of a million dollars. How could I not have known? Every year, I signed our joint tax return after he filled it out, and only saw the bottom line, which wasn't that much.

When I finished reading, I leaned back against my pillows and struggled with conflicting thoughts. David had instilled in me the idea of self-responsibility, and I tried to see how I had gotten myself to this point. How had I skewed things enough to allow my husband to take such advantage of me? Now I had a decision to make. Should I let him 'take me to the cleaners' as Jay had said, or should I fight back? What would the angel advise now?

I closed my eyes, remembering that David had told me to listen and I would hear his voice. Taking several deep breaths and letting them out, I became quiet and truly tried to listen for his wise words. They came, just as he said they would.

Being responsible for your own actions, does not mean letting others take advantage of you. It doesn't mean you should become a doormat. It does mean doing the right thing, the decent thing.

"And what is that?" I asked.

Remember that revenge only serves to reward the avenger for a temporary time. Do nothing for the sake of getting even. However, justice is a different matter. Robert's selfish attempt to keep you from having anything he considers his is unjust. The right thing would be to secure your future without endangering his.

Then he was gone. No matter how hard I tried to make contact, no matter how much I asked, David seemed to have disappeared. I had to rely on what he had said and figure out just how to go about doing it.

CHAPTER NINE

ON CAMERA

ROBERT CAME HOME on Friday, and then only to change clothes and leave a load of laundry. Until he walked in and saw me, I don't think he even realized I had left the hospital.

Alex and I depended heavily on Mattie Washington, the housekeeper he had hired, for our daily sustenance. I still couldn't get around very well, and Mattie cooked, cleaned, and pampered the two of us. For once, at least, Robert had made a wise decision.

On Sunday, I decided to check out the beach house in Malibu. Good old Moira helped me search through drawers and closets, and we finally came up with three keys that looked like they might fit a front door. When we found the place, we felt like burglars casing the joint.

"What if Robert and that bimbo are in there?" I said.

"We'll yell *surprise*! Think we should have brought a cake?"

I loved the way she lightened my mood. "Anything for a party, hm?"

"Sure, why not?"

"I don't see his car."

"Or hers."

"Maybe inside the garage." I chickened out. "Let's just go home."

"Not on your life, babe. I'm having too much fun."

Moira stalked up to the door and inserted one of the keys, then another. The third opened the lock. She swung the door wide and yelled, "Hello! Anybody home?"

The place was silent. I felt like an intruder, but tiptoed as best I could on crutches through the rooms.

"This is the house I've always dreamed of having," I breathed. "Almost every window has a view of the water." I hated Robert for keeping the place a secret.

A wonderful, wooden deck ran the length of the house. I imagined sitting there in the early morning, a cup of coffee in my hand, watching sea gulls dive for their breakfast. Maybe Jonathan Livingston Seagull would approach and let me in on some of his wisdom. I made a decision.

"I'm going to tell Jay I want this house. Robert can have the apartments and his pension. He'll have to split the money and stocks with me so I can maintain this place and support my mission."

"Mission?"

"You know. What David said I had to do."

"Oh, yeah. And have you decided how?"

I sank down on the plush, white couch and gazed out at the breakers pounding the sandy beach. "Hell, no. But once things are settled and my body is back to normal, I'll have time to plan."

Robert flew into a rage when he received a letter from Irene Turner which set out my demands, especially my request for spousal support. He caved in, however, when my attorney mentioned that forgery was a punishable crime. Irene had assured me that I was being more than fair, and something told me she was right. If the judge agreed, there would be a just division of property.

Alex decided she wanted to live in the family home with her father, until she went away to college and could live on her own. At first, I was devastated that she would prefer him to me, but she explained it had nothing to do with either of us. At this time in her life, friends were more important than parents. She wanted to be near them, especially since she'd be leaving for Berkeley in the fall. I realized that was only a few short weeks away, and Alex would probably be more comfortable in the house where she grew up anyway, at least until Rita Dunn worked her magic and closed escrow. The sad part was that Robert didn't want her there.

"What difference does it make, Robert?" I said. "It's only for a short time, and Mattie will care for her. You've been spending most of your time at Nikki's, anyway. Nothing will change except that I'll be someplace else, and you'll have to extend the closing a few days."

"A mother should have custody."

"We'll have joint custody, both physical and legal."

"You seem to think you're going to get your way on this, don't you?"

Was that a whine I heard in his voice? All of a sudden, I realized how much he sounded like a little boy. I fought the impulse to think of myself as a bully or as his mother. Instead, I passed the responsibility right back to him.

"Alex is my main concern, and she should be yours, too. Where she lives isn't that important. Mattie won't let her stay out late or have boys in her bedroom. I'll look in on her nearly every day, and you will, too." I cocked an eyebrow. "Won't you?"

"I'm busy."

"Too busy to be a father?" I appealed to his material side. "Besides, you won't have to pay me child support this way."

Every objection Robert came up with, I answered. I couldn't believe how strong I sounded.

Without asking for permission, I moved my things into the beach house and changed the locks. Before too long, my doctor told me I could start living a normal life. It felt good to get behind the wheel of a car again. Pushing my own grocery cart down the aisle while I shopped was a pleasure. No longer an invalid, I began to mull over ideas about how to spread David's word before I forgot everything he had told me.

One evening, Jay and Moira came to dinner.

"What about television?" Jay said. He speared a piece of beef and raised it. "Every cable company has to provide a public access channel."

"Public access? What's that?"

Since Jay had just filled his mouth with steak, Moira took over the task of explaining. "They give you a class on how to produce a show and even provide you with all the equipment you need and a staff of people, who are interns or students or something, but who know pretty much what they're doing."

"How do you know so much about it?"

Jay swallowed and gave his wife a loving look. "Moira just produced a show herself."

Moira beamed. "I'm selling vitamins and herbs over the internet, and my show tells which ones do what for your body. I'm doing so well, I'm thinking about incorporating."

I felt hurt. "You never said a word to me about this."

"You needed to concentrate on getting well. I didn't want to take any of your time away from that."

"Well, your heart may have been in the right place, but I'm really upset with you."

Admitting this to her was a major step for me. I had always kept my anger to myself. My accidental brush with death had convinced me how important it is to say what I feel. I might never get another chance.

Moira looked confused. "I thought I was doing the right thing."

I smiled. "It's okay, my friend. Just don't ever keep me in the dark about something that means so much to you. If it's important to you, then it is to me, as well. Now, tell me more about public access television."

By the end of the evening, Moira had agreed to be my producer and promised to schedule two half-hour segments. In about ten days, I would be a television star. Or so I hoped.

"I'm really nervous," I admitted as we sat in the cable company's *green room* waiting to begin our taping.

Moira had brought donuts. "I was told the crew works better if they're well fed."

She fiddled around, arranging them on a plastic platter. She stayed quiet for so long, I wondered what was wrong. Moira is never at a loss for words.

"What's on your mind?" I said.

"Nothing."

"Don't give me that."

She stopped what she was doing and came to sit beside me. "Do you even know what you're going to say? I don't see any notes. You haven't given me any words to scroll from the teleprompter. I'm worried you'll get out there and fall on your face. I mean, it's not a live audience or anything, but once we start, we can't stop. I had my whole infomercial scripted; it's the only way I could have done it."

I held out my hands to show her how badly I was shaking. "You're right. I don't know what I'm going to say. When I meditated this morning, David's voice told me to wing it, that I'd be fine."

Moira shook her head. "That's okay for a pro, honey bunch, but this is your first venture into TV."

"Yeah, well, it's too late to do anything else now."

As if on cue, a roly-poly young man with dark, curly hair that fell over his forehead, poked his head through the open doorway. "Time, ladies. You've got twenty minutes to light the joint."

Moira arranged a high-back chair and small side table on the set, and placed a green plant on the table. "Sit, honey."

I did as I was told and waited while she and the crew lit the back drop and then me. When they finished, I ran to the bathroom and threw up. Cold, wet paper towels on the back of my neck revived me, but the swirling in my stomach wouldn't stop. "I can't do this," I said to my image in the mirror. A voice in my head replied. *Of course you can. You're going to be wonderful.*

I sat in my chair on stage and waited until Moira pointed a finger at me. I took a deep breath and began. "Hello," I said. "I'm Paxton Michaels, and I'm here to tell you a strange story. Perhaps you'll believe me, but maybe you won't. It doesn't really matter as long as you listen and, hopefully, find some truth in what I am about to say."

I left out the part about my philandering husband, and started with the accident. I told about flying towards the light and finding an angel waiting there. I talked about coming out of my coma and discovering that no one believed me. Then I began to teach. The words came easily, so easily that I couldn't attribute them to what was going on inside my own brain. I felt as though some extraordinary power was speaking through me, using my voice. I was so open that I seemed to be in touch with all the wisdom of the universe.

"There are those of you who have been searching to find your purpose in life. I'm here to tell you that you have only one purpose, and that is to learn your Divine Nature. If you don't think you are Divine, let me provide an analogy that may clear things up for you.

"You have a mother and father—two people whose sperm and egg became a human being. Literally, you *are* your parents. One cell from each person combined to become you. In the same way, they are their parents, and their parents before them. Every ancestor you have ever had still exists in you.

"If you believe the Bible, you learned that, in the beginning, there was nothing but God. If there was nothing else, then God must have created everything out of Itself, out of some kind of Divine Substance, you might say. Therefore, everything God created, in a manner of speaking, *is* God.

"Just as you are your parents and your grandparents, you can also say that you are God. That means you have every quality of the divine as part of your makeup. You have the ability to love, for one thing. And you can create your own world of experience.

"You choose where to live, what to eat, the words you're going to say, who your friends are. More importantly, you create your response to situations and circumstances. You draw to yourself people who either love or hate you. Every thought you think, every word you utter, and every act you perform serves as the catalyst for something to happen. 'Do unto others as you would have them do unto you' isn't simply a suggestion on how to get what you want, but a warning. You really do get back what you give out. For every action, there is a reaction.

"Most of the time, you create unconsciously, because you haven't yet realized that you have a choice. Know this then. You do."

I listened to my inner voice for a moment, then continued. "Here's something else to consider. To create your world or to change it, you don't even have to believe in God. You only have to have an awareness that there is something powerful within you that is greater than you could ever imagine it to be. It isn't something you can detect with your five senses, it doesn't have depth or breadth or weight, but it is a part of you, and you can use it. How? By consciously choosing what you want in life rather than being subject to circumstance. Declare what you want and live as though you already have it."

The time passed quickly, and I crammed a lot of information into my talk. When I finally finished, I smiled at the camera while the credits rolled. As soon as the camera light went off, Moira flew at me and gave me a hug. "You're awesome, baby doll."

One of the camera operators scowled at me. "Do you really believe that stuff?" he said.

I thought for a moment and then answered as honestly as I could. "I'm beginning to."

CHAPTER TEN

MAIL CALL

I HAD JUST emerged from the shower and was toweling my hair dry when the phone rang.

"Hello?"

"Mrs. Michaels?"

"Yes, this is she."

"This is Rory Jacobs from Public Access. I thought you might like to know you've had some fan mail."

"Fan mail?"

"As a result of your show. Got a few letters responding to it. It's been shown three times, and now you've got mail."

"That's amazing. Can you forward it to me?"

"Well, there's quite a bit here. We'd prefer that you'd come in and pick it up. I can leave it at the front desk, if you want to come today. I'll put your tapes with the mail. You might want to take them to some of the other cable stations. They'll be happy to air them for you."

"Thanks. I'll be there around one."

I was stunned, never dreaming that people would write to me after listening to what I'd said. Would the letters be supportive? Or was I going to be coming home with a handful of hate mail? There was only one way to find out.

Parking was at a premium at the station, but I managed to find a space near the front door - a good thing as I was soon to find out.

"Hi," I said to the receptionist. "I'm Paxton Michaels. I believe you have some mail for me."

"Oh, gosh, Mrs. Michaels, we sure do. I hope you'll bring your tapes back so we can air them again in a few weeks. I missed seeing your show, but after what I heard about it, I won't miss it the next time. Will you need some help out to the car?"

"No, I think I can handle it."

"Well, if you're sure..."

The young woman dragged a canvas bag from behind the counter and deposited it in front of me. "It's pretty heavy," she said.

I couldn't believe my eyes. "Are you sure all this is for me?"

"Every bit of it."

"Then maybe I will need some help."

The receptionist made a quick phone call and a burly man with tattoos on his arms soon appeared. He hoisted the bag on his shoulder and followed me to my recently purchased 2001 Honda.

"I saw your show," he said as he flipped the bag into the trunk. "Are you speaking anywhere? I'd like to bring some friends to hear you."

"Um, well, no. I haven't got any speaking engagements planned."

"When you do, will you put me on your mailing list?" He pulled a scrap of paper from his jeans pocket, jotted down a note, and handed it to me. "That's my address."

I glanced at the information he had written. "Okay, uh, Peter. I'll do that." I held out my hand. "Thanks for your help."

The drive back to Malibu was far too long. I couldn't wait to open the bag and begin reading. When I reached the house, I called Moira.

"You won't believe what has happened!" I explained about the mound of mail that still sat in my car. "I'll have to bring it in a little bit at a time. The bag weighs a ton."

"You'll need a secretary just to help you sift through it," Moira said. "Want me to come over later and help read?"

"Would you?"

"Of course, honey bunch. I'm as curious as you are. Pencil me in for five o'clock. You can serve me dinner since Jay has to work late."

By the time Moira arrived, I'd gotten through about a third of the letters and post cards. I had two piles sitting on my living room floor. The larger one was mostly complimentary, from people who wanted to know more. The other was filled with hate. Several people even threatened me, saying I didn't deserve to live. Many thought I was a tool of the devil. A few offered to de-program me, figuring I'd fallen under the evil influences of a cult. How could talking about living with integrity disturb so many people?

"Look at this, Moira. Who would ever believe there is such a wide gap between these two piles?"

"Polarity," she said.

"I don't understand."

"You have an extreme opinion at one end of the pole and a second, almost radical belief at the other end. The funny part is that they are about the same thing."

"God."

"Yep. Or religion."

"And neither is wrong, just a different view. Maybe what I have to do is find a way to integrate the two."

"Good luck, sweetie pie."

We read for another hour, tossing letters into their appropriate piles. Finally, Moira complained. "I thought you were fixing dinner for us. My tummy's growling like crazy."

"You're right. We need to take a break. I made a big pot of vegetable soup and baked some bread."

"Sounds fabulous. I'll get the bowls."

"I'll slice the bread."

"Did you churn some butter, too?"

"I'm not that much of a home-body," I said, laughing. "But I do have the real thing. I know you're not a margarine type of person."

Sort of like love, I thought. Moira went for the real thing. I managed to squeak by on an imitation.

Moira squinted and cocked her head. "Actually, I expected pizza. I figured this new image of yours didn't include home cooking."

I thought about that before answering. "I'm making some shifts in my life, but most of the time, change comes slowly. Sudden metamorphosis scares me."

"As it does most people. The other day, Jay asked two secretaries to switch desks. The change was absolutely logical. It put them in closer proximity to their bosses. You'd have thought he asked them to move to another planet."

"It's no wonder people resist. But when you think about it, making a conscious effort to do things differently is the only way we grow."

"Great attitude, kiddo. Wish I could embrace that philosophy a little more fully."

"Well," I said, "one thing hasn't changed. It's nearly seven o'clock, and my stomach says it's time to eat. I always eat by seven. Habit? Or necessity? I'm not willing to change, regardless."

"Thank goodness! Dish out that soup and let's get started."

Moira had a stack of letters in her hand and placed them on the table. She ladled hot soup into bowls while I extracted warm sourdough from my bread-maker and put a square of butter on a plate. We sat across from each other and grinned as we took our first bites.

"Yum," Moira said. "At least some things don't change. You're still a terrific chef. Or is it cheffess?"

After a few spoonsful of soup, I couldn't resist and reached for the letter on top of the stack Moira had brought to the table.

"This one looks official. Computer label. Printed stationery." I read the return address. "Carl and Lydia Martin from Bel Air. Even the rich folks watch poor man's TV."

I opened the envelope and began to read. "Listen to this. *Dear Ms. Michaels: We took great interest in your recent program taped for Public Access Television. As promoters of talent, we also have a desire to present new ideas to the public which have the potential to change lives. Your convictions appear to fall into the category we are seeking to publicize at this time. Please call us at the number listed below if you are interested in discussing this matter further.* Moira, maybe this is just what I need. An agent. Two agents, actually. Someone working to get my story out there."

"Whoa, there, honey bunch. You don't know anything about these people." She took the paper from my hand. "This address looks like a private residence, not a business. Wouldn't professional agents have an office?"

I felt deflated. "I suppose so. But it wouldn't hurt to talk to them, would it?"

She scanned the letter again, shaking her head. Then she shrugged. "I guess not. Just don't sign anything without running it by Jay first, okay?"

"I promise. But admit it, Moira, it's kind of exciting to think I could have an agent paving the way for me, setting up speaking engagements, maybe interviews." I preened a bit. "Can you imagine me on the Oprah Show?"

"Hmm, she does air some pretty weird stuff."

"Weird stuff?" I said, feeling defensive. "Do you think my ideas are weird?"

"No, just different. As a matter of fact, I've been thinking a lot about what you said at your taping. Like it or not, I'm beginning to believe it myself. So call and make an appointment with the Martins. If you want me to come along, I will."

"No, I need to do this myself. I'll phone tomorrow. In the meantime, how about some apple crumb cake?"

Moira pretended to wipe drool from her chin. "Lead me to it, honey bunch. Feed me sweets and I'll be your slave for life."

CHAPTER ELEVEN

THE MARTINS

AS IT TURNED out, Carl and Lydia Martin had an office on Little Santa Monica in Beverly Hills. It was a tiny hole-in-the-wall with two desks, a computer, and a few folding chairs. I was not impressed. However, the Martins, themselves, were quite imposing.

Carl stood about six-feet-seven. His white hair was long enough to flow over the collar of his Armani suit. He wore a ruby ring on his left pinky and a diamond stud in his right ear.

Lydia reminded me of a cross between a red-headed Dolly Parton and the wife of a defrocked televangelist. Her eyelashes overpowered her shapely but diminutive figure, and her three-inch heels only served to bring the top of her poofy hairdo up to mid-chest on her husband. Diamonds were her jewelry of choice, and she wore a lot of them.

Carl spoke with a Boston accent, and Lydia must have been born someplace in Georgia. They seemed as opposite as day and night, and I wondered how they had ever gotten together. Their only common interest, at first glance, was their love of quality clothing and expensive jewelry.

We shook hands, and Carl apologized for the appearance of the office. "We like to keep things simple here," he said. "If we look too prosperous, people tend to think we're making too much money and try to talk us down in what we'll take for our clients' services."

His sense of logic escaped me. The frugal office was such a sharp contrast to their flamboyant dress that it only served to point out where they preferred to spend their money and would never convince anyone they lived a Spartan existence.

"I'm eager to hear your proposal, Mr. Martin," I said.

"Carl, please. And my wife is Lydia. Let's not be formal, Paxton."

I preferred a more business-like relationship, but the Martins obviously liked the friendly approach.

"Thank you... Carl." I sat on one of the folding chairs. "Your letter didn't give many details. Can you tell me what you have in mind?"

Carl adjusted his gem-studded cufflinks. "My wife and I believe that your philosophy is the coming thing for the new millennium. People are ready for change and some of your ideas are, shall we say, fodder for radical transformation. We'd like to arrange a speaking tour for you."

"A tour? You mean I'd have to go on the road?"

"In a manner of speaking."

Lydia gushed with enthusiasm. "Why, Paxton, it would be a perfect venue for you. You seemed so comfortable speaking to the camera. A live audience wouldn't be much different."

How could she connect the two? Looking out at a hundred people was a *lot* different. Cameras are inanimate objects. People heckle and ask questions.

"I don't know, Lydia. I'm not exactly wild about the idea. You must realize I have no experience with public speaking."

"We'd be right there with you providing direction and guidance."

"You'd go on tour with me? You have that kind of time? What about your other clients?"

Carl chuckled. "We rarely take on more than one client at a time. When we promote someone, we *promote* him or her. We'll teach you how to dress, how to speak and gesture, how to get an audience eating out of your hand. When you're ready, we'll do the advertising and get the people there."

"Goodness. This sounds like an expensive proposition. How much would I have to pay you?"

The Martins glanced at each other and smiled. "Absolutely nothing," Carl said. "Our fee would be a percentage of whatever you took in on tour."

"You mean we'd charge people to hear me? I don't think I can do that."

Lydia and Carl looked horrified.

"Not charge?" Carl said.

Lydia's soft, southern accent turned persuasive. "What would be your objection to a minimal admission fee, darling? Every good speaker does it."

"My message is for everyone, not just for those who can afford to hear it. I want the poorest of poor to know they have a chance for a better life."

Carl started to object, but Lydia held up her hand, and he shut up.

"I totally understand," she said. "I suppose we could simply take a collection so that people would only have to pay what they could. One person might drop a fifty into the plate and the homeless person next to him might pass the plate on without putting anything in at all. What do you think of that idea?"

"I'm not sure."

"We'd only have to meet our expenses."

"Then how would you make any money?"

"Our fee would be part of the expenses. We'll take care of everything. If we don't take in enough money, we will pay the difference out of our own pocket."

This sounded too good to be true. "Why?"

"Because what you have to say is far too important not to get it out there to the masses."

Carl chimed in. "Lydia's right. Besides, I'm confident that people will be generous. What do you say, little lady?"

Things were moving too fast. I wasn't certain I was ready for this. "I'll have to think about it. I'm just not sure..."

Carl smiled, reaching across the desk to pat my hand. "Take your time. We'll call you in a couple days to see if you have any questions. In the meantime, Lydia and I will draw up a contract outlining everything we can do for you and what we need from you in return."

"I'd want my attorney to look at it, of course."

The couple exchanged a look. "Of course," Lydia said. "We would expect you to consult a lawyer."

"However," Carl said, "don't wait too long. If you don't want to do this, we need to be moving on to the next client."

He stood and moved toward the door, officially dismissing me. Suddenly, I began to panic. What if no one else wanted to help me? "Send me the contract. I'll have an answer for you in a few days."

I wrote down my home address and phone number, then left.

"I don't know what to make of them, Moira," I said, pushing around the lettuce on my plate. "They seem anxious to represent me, but not so eager that they wouldn't feel comfortable turning their backs on me and going on to someone else."

She finished chewing a bite of shrimp cocktail before answering. "What bothers me is that they have no other clients. Don't you think you should ask for references?"

"That's a good idea. I'll call them this afternoon."

And I did. Carl seemed happy to comply and gave me the number for a man he had just finished working with on a film.

"Boyd Perkins? I don't think I've heard of him."

"You will, little lady. You will. This is his first picture, but the producers are ecstatic. They're calling him the next Nicholas Cage."

"Really? That's wonderful. How did you represent him?"

"Introduced him to the right people. Kept on their tails until they auditioned him. One screen test, and he was in like Flynn. Poor guy was worried that he was getting too old and would have to give up acting before he got his big chance. He's nearly thirty and you know how it is in the industry."

Actually, I didn't, but I agreed to call Boyd and talk with him. Later, I dialed the number and got his machine.

"Hi, this is Boyd. If you're expecting a return call soon, you're in for a disappointment. I'm off to Calgary to re-shoot a few scenes from my movie. Then I'm off to Scotland for a month. Leave your number and I'll call you when I get back."

Disappointment was too mild a word. I really felt the need to talk to this man and find out if he was satisfied with the Martins' representation. I left my name and number, saying that I hoped he'd pick up the message early and call me collect. Then I got the bright idea of asking Lydia and Carl for the location number. I called them, but got another machine.

"Lydia and I are off for a short sabbatical before taking on a new client. Leave your message at the beep, and we'll call you when we return from New York."

Frustrated, I wondered how they could have packed up so quickly. They must have had the trip planned before I met with them. Obviously, they weren't hurting for money if they could vacation and not worry about where their next client was coming from.

The contract arrived two days later. I read through it and found nothing that seemed objectionable. Jay Plunkett took another couple of days to go over it.

"It seems pretty straight forward," he said when I met with him. "They'll arrange a 20-city tour over twelve months, do all the advertising with no up-front fees from you, and they only get paid if you make a profit. On paper, it looks ideal." He seemed worried.

"So what's the problem?"

"I don't know." He handed the papers to me. "Something doesn't ring true, but I can't find anything that would give you any reason to reject it. Maybe it's because I've never read an agency agreement that was so one-sided toward the client."

"But that's a good thing, right?"

"Right."

"Do you think I should tear it up?"

He shook his head. "No. Just be careful. Keep your fingers in the pie. Don't turn everything over to them without asking questions. Know what they're doing at all times. Remember, you're the client."

"I'm in control."

"Yep."

"I'll remember that."

That night, when I sat alone on my deck listening to the waves lap the shore, I asked for guidance.

"God, let me know what to do. Give me a sign. Should I go with the Martins? Just how far am I supposed to take this message that David saddled me with?" I realized I was feeling sorry for myself. "And please make me feel good about what I'm doing."

The skies didn't open up and thunder didn't roll. David didn't speak in my head. No one called with an inspiring message. The moon created a line of light on the water, and a straggler gull flew home to wherever seagulls go after dark. The decision had to be mine. No guiding spirit would decide for me.

"Damned choices!" I yelled into the night.

CHAPTER TWELVE

ON THE ROAD

THREE WEEKS LATER, my bags were packed and I sat with the Martins at the American Airlines terminal waiting for the call to board our plane.

"You're fidgeting," Lydia said. "Are you afraid to fly, darling?"

"No," I replied.

She placed her hand on my jiggling knee. "Well, you certainly seem nervous about something."

"Nervous isn't the half of it. I'm scared to death. Are you sure I'm ready for this? I mean, after all, I've never been in front of a live audience before. How many people did you say would be there?"

Carl patted my other knee, which made me even more fidgety. "There, there, little lady, you'll be just fine. I keep telling you we booked you for a small group for the first time out. Only about 50 people."

Lydia tried to be comforting. "Phoenix is a progressive city, lots of metaphysical churches and new thought groups. You'll be welcome there."

Her husband nodded. "Absolutely. And we're not charging a cent."

"Right," Lydia said. "The group is a non-profit society. They're asking a nominal fee for the tickets and giving us a percentage as a donation."

I sighed. Alex was off shopping for school clothes, getting ready for her freshman year in college. I felt like I should be with her instead of traipsing around the country. My only hope for justifying the trip was that I had finally begun doing the work David had assigned me.

"There's our boarding call," Carl said.

I listened to the voice over the loud speaker. "First class?"

Lydia smiled. "We always travel first class. Believe me, you'll love it."

Of course, I'd love it. I had always wanted to sit in those wider seats at the front of the plane. Robert never thought it warranted the extra fare, although he flew first class when a client or his company paid. It worried me that the Martins would end up taking money from their own pocket to pay for these plush accommodations.

"Where are we staying?"

"A very nice hotel, darling."

Lydia gathered her things and headed for the gate, effectively barring further conversation for the time being. Carl and I followed, cutting in front of other people lined up waiting for their turn to board. I averted my eyes, half expecting to see indignant looks on their faces. Silly, I guess. I never thought anything bad about first class passengers when

I traveled in coach. Well, maybe there was a little jealousy. The idea of anyone envying me was surprising.

Lydia graciously gave me the window seat, and Carl took up two seats across the aisle. Within moments, we each held a crystal flute filled with bubbling champagne. Such service!

Lydia promptly donned headphones and began tapping her polished acrylics on the arm rest in time to music I couldn't hear. Had she isolated herself this way to keep me from questioning her further about our *gig*, as Alex called it? She wore the headphones all the way to Phoenix, even through a hastily served lunch.

When we disembarked, I spied a chubby, older woman sporting a sign that read, *Paxton Michaels.*

"Look, someone is waiting for us."

Carl's gaze followed my pointing finger. "Mmm, our hosts' idea of a chauffeur, apparently." He didn't look pleased.

I waved to the woman, smiled, and pointed to myself. She practically jumped up and down with joy and hurried to where we stood.

"Oh, Miss Michaels, I'm so glad I found you. I got here an hour ago, just to make sure I wouldn't miss your plane in case it came in early." She grabbed my hand and shook it vigorously. "I'm Edna Conklin, president of the New Millennium Society. Goodness, but we're glad you agreed to come."

"Let me introduce you to my managers," I said, indicating my traveling companions. "Carl and Lydia Martin."

They greeted Edna with little enthusiasm, but Edna retained her happy demeanor. "How wonderful to meet you," she said. "I have a car waiting."

Carl's voice sounded haughty. "We were expecting a limousine."

Edna laughed. "Why would we rent one of those things when I have a perfectly good Volkswagen bus that'll hold just about any amount of luggage you might come up with? It's ten years old, but runs great. You go down to Baggage Claim and get your bags. I'll get the car and meet you out front. Take your time. I don't mind waiting."

Edna scurried off, looking back twice to wave and nod. Carl and Lydia seemed furious.

"This was not part of our contract," Carl said.

Lydia scowled. "You should have let me read it first."

They bickered as we walked, each trying to blame the lack of a limo on the other. Finally, I intervened.

"Excuse me, but does it really matter that one of the group's members is driving us to the hotel instead of a chauffeur? Isn't it enough that we don't have to take a cab?"

Lydia practically whined. "But we have to get our own luggage."

"I don't know about you, but to me, that's a minor inconvenience. I'll rent one of those carts, and we can pile all of our bags on it. Or get a porter to take it. The tip is on me, in that case. If you make any more of this, I'll be very upset; and when I'm upset, I can't think of a thing to say. Surely, you don't want me to get up on stage and be tongue tied."

Without thinking, I had said exactly the right thing to make the Martins shut up. I handed a skycap ten dollars, and he pulled our bags from the carousel and wheeled everything out to the curb. Edna saw us and waved. Within minutes, we were slicing across traffic and headed toward the exit.

Our driver kept up a running conversation, pointing out the sights as we sped along. "I've lived here all my life," she said, "and that's more than sixty years if you couldn't tell."

Lydia and Carl exchanged a glance, and I gave them a warning look. I didn't want them spoiling this friendly woman's day.

Edna continued. "Hope you can stand the weather. The TV says we're due for a heat wave starting tomorrow. Up to now, it's been in the high seventies, low eighties, but look out, triple digit degrees ahead. Did you bring your bathing suits? The motel has a pool."

This got Carl's attention. "Motel?"

"Yep. Four Star Motel on Franklin. Just like you said."

"I said a four-star hotel."

Edna's face clouded. "Oops. I guess somebody misunderstood." She brightened. "But, hey, the Four Star is a nice place. We got you the best rooms in the house, and there's a Denny's right next door so you can grab breakfast."

"This is totally unacceptable," Lydia said.

"Actually, it's quite acceptable."

The Martins looked at me.

"I mean it. If you had consulted me beforehand, I would not have agreed to spending money on posh accommodations."

Edna interrupted. "Don't worry, Ms. Michaels. We don't mind the expense."

This was news to me. "You're paying for the rooms?"

Carl answered for her. "That's part of our agreement."

I turned to Edna. "You're a non-profit group, right?"

"That's right."

"I used to volunteer for a couple non-profits, and I know how tight money can be. If I'm not mistaken, you probably hope to come out ahead with the money you bring in for my lecture."

Edna grimaced and glanced at Carl. "Not really. There won't be much...."

"They get a percentage, just like us," Carl interjected. "Not to worry. We'll stay at the Four Star and make the best of it."

Lydia agreed somewhat reluctantly. "Of course."

I vowed to read any further contracts before agreeing to another trip.

The Four Star Motel wasn't half-bad to my way of thinking. Our rooms overlooked the pool, and we each had a private, tree-shaded balcony with a little table and two chairs. Edna insisted on helping to carry our bags to our rooms.

"I'll pick you up at seven for dinner. We want you to meet some of our more prestigious members." She toodle-ooed and scampered off.

That left me a couple of hours to soak in a tub and relax. I told my grim-faced companions I needed some quiet time and that I'd call them when I was ready.

I often bathed by candlelight at home, and had brought several candles and some lavender bath salts with me. It seemed important to maintain the ritual, since it soothed me and allowed time for occasional mental conversations with my angel friend.

I sank into the scented water and released the tension created by the Martins' quibbling. Aloud, I said, "Please let this be the right thing to do."

What is right and what is wrong? What you're doing is merely...

"A choice. See? You're predictable, David."

No, you're just learning to think as I do.

"I suppose that's a good thing?"

I'd like to think it is.

"David, what am I going to say to these people?

You'll know when the time comes.

He had a lot more confidence in me than I had in myself. The tension returned and, by the time Edna knocked on my door, I had a headache that Tylenol ® could barely dent.

Edna seemed excited. "George Peabody is coming to dinner with us, and he's agreed to pick up the tab. You'll love George. He's our wealthiest member—a criminal lawyer who makes beaucoup bucks defending innocent people who have been accused of crimes."

I gave her an inquiring look over the top edge of my sunglasses.

Edna's eyes twinkled, as though she could read my mind. "At least, they're deemed innocent by the juries George persuades."

This woman had a lot more on the ball than Lydia and Carl gave her credit for.

We picked up the Martins at their door, and Edna chauffeured us to Vincenzo's Little Italy in her bus. The odor of garlic assailed our senses the moment we walked through the door.

A tuxedoed maitre d' greeted us. "Welcome to Vincenzo's."

"Vinnie, this is Paxton Michaels," Edna said. "She's our guest speaker for tomorrow."

Vinnie. This must be the owner of the establishment.

"Belissimo!" he said, kissing his fingers. Then he bowed and kissed my hand. "I'm looking forward to hearing what you have to say." He ignored the Martins, much to their annoyance.

Vinnie showed us to a table where four other people waited. Edna introduced George Peabody and his wife, Joan, and another couple, Sarah and Frank Steele. The Steeles were ancient, wrinkled and deaf. Luckily, Edna seemed content to sit next to them, repeating most of what I said throughout the evening so I didn't have to shout.

George shook my hand with a firm but gentle grip and indicated that I should sit across from him. "So glad to meet you, my dear." He acknowledged Carl and Lydia, then seemed to forget they were there.

The little group made me feel comfortable as we got to know each other. It wasn't until dessert that Sarah Steele brought the conversation around to my impending lecture.

"Will you be discussing UFOs by any chance?"

"UFOs?"

"You'll have to forgive Sarah," George said. "She was abducted by aliens in 1963 and hasn't been able to talk about anything else since then."

"Oh, my," said Lydia.

Oh, my, indeed. What had I gotten myself into?

CHAPTER THIRTEEN

THE NEW MILLENNIUM SOCIETY

DESPITE SARAH STEELE'S preoccupation with flying saucers, the majority of the society's members were normal people with an interest in new or alternative methods to make their lives work better. True to their word, they filled the room with a few more than fifty people, who sat with eagerness obvious on their smiling faces. I had half-expected condemnation and skepticism, and their openness put me at ease.

After Edna introduced me, I stood at the lectern and merely told my story, just as I had done on video tape. When I explained that the first lesson to be learned is that life is about choice, heads in the audience nodded in agreement. Then I decided to try something new, hoping David would help.

"Rather than standing here lecturing, why don't you ask me questions. I'll try to answer them to the best of my ability."

For a moment, I thought I had made a mistake when there was silence. Finally, George Peabody broke the ice.

"Because of my profession as a criminal lawyer, I often defend the dregs of society—

thieves, rapists, murderers. Sometimes, I feel like I'm dealing with the devil himself. Still, I often see some good in even the foulest of personalities. Tell us what David might say about that."

It wasn't David's words that inspired me, but an earlier conversation with Moira about polarity. I turned to a dry-erase board Edna had provided in case I wanted to make an illustration and drew a straight line. "Maybe I can answer that in a roundabout way." At one end of the line, I wrote *Hot.* At the other, I marked *Cold.*

"If you look at these as different degrees of the same thing, you have to wonder about what's in between." I indicated the middle of the line. "At what point does hot become cold? For that matter, when does high become low or right become wrong? Even with righteousness and evil, there is a spot where good and bad are a matter of interpretation.

"How many of you will say that absolute honesty is imperative to live life with integrity?"

Everyone in the room held up a hand.

"And who of you has been guilty of telling a child about Santa Claus or the tooth fairy? Have you turned in an expense account and rounded the mileage up just a tad? Did you ever use a restroom at McDonald's when their sign said 'For Customers Only', and then left without buying even a cup of coffee? Perhaps you rationalized it by thinking that, on occasion, you have purchased something there?"

A great many in the audience squirmed in their seats or looked guiltily at their neighbors.

"Are you evil? I think not. Are you totally righteous?" I shook my head. "You are simply being human, trying to be the best person you can be. You see, it is here in the middle between the distinctly black and white areas, where good and bad are muddled in grey, that most of us live our lives. And it is in this indistinct place that choice becomes important. Sometimes you make choices that are to the right of center; sometimes a little to the left. Each time you make a decision that leans to the side of wrong, it becomes a little easier to do it again.

"The man who kills, whether it is in anger or for personal gain, or even if it is for the thrill of it, has made an abhorrent choice, one that the majority would say is unacceptable at the least, and a sin against God at the most."

A woman stood and asked, "Don't you think a killer is evil?"

I thought for a moment and prayed that the right intent would come through me. I was getting in pretty deep here, and hoped I wasn't about to drown in my own words.

"I hate to start talking about God, because some of you might be atheists or have a pretty set notion about what God is or is not. Nevertheless, this may be the only way I can answer your question.

"Is a killer evil? If the thing that created us is pure and good and loving, then I don't believe it can know anything about evil and doesn't recognize it in its creation. Man created the concept of iniquity and gave it authority, because he believes in duality and gives credence to the idea that there is a power in the Universe other than God. So, no, I don't believe the person committing the crime is evil. He or she is simply making a terrible choice and will someday, somehow suffer the consequences."

The same woman rose again. "You mean he'll go to hell."

"Not at all. Hell isn't a place to go."

I wasn't just saying that. After spending time with David, it was something I instinctively knew. But how?

"He may *sense* hell from his misdeeds, but it will be within him. I've read about near-death episodes where the person experiences all of the things he has done to others and feels their pain. But it is temporary, not an eternal damnation. The spiral of life is always upwards, and we are given chance after chance to move in that direction."

A tall man with a Jamaican accent said, "Perhaps you will address the issue of the so-called bad seed? Or the crack baby. Both of these individuals will be more likely to make harmful decisions. But are they responsible for their choices?"

"At some point, we are all responsible for our choices. David told me we agree to be born to certain parents or with certain conditions because we want to learn something about life. Or teach something."

"Do we come back again? I'm talking about reincarnation."

"I don't know. But if we do, I suspect that it would only be with the intent of evolving forward, not backward."

George Peabody spoke again. "What about the victim? Surely he didn't choose to be killed."

"Of course not. But if he had a belief in the possibility of *anyone* being murdered, then he also believed it was a possibility in his own life. His belief was his choice."

Another man interjected. "That's crazy. The news is full of all kinds of terrible things. When we see it, how can we not believe it?"

"You can acknowledge the belief as man-created and then reject it. Look beyond the appearance of the act and remember that the same beauty and perfection which created you, created the criminal as well. Realize that Spirit is in the midst of everything that happens, no matter what it looks like."

I sounded like an evangelist. As I expected, not everyone was in agreement. People started grumbling amongst themselves. It was time to change the subject. Unfortunately, it was Sally Steele who seemed to agree with me. I cringed when she stood and adjusted her hearing aids.

"Do you believe in life on other planets?"

It wasn't my intention to stir up any more controversy than I already had. "Probably not on the planets that surround our sun. But who am I to say that we are the only life-sustaining unit in the entire universe?"

"I was abducted by aliens, you know."

"I've heard that about you, Sally. And I'm sure your story is interesting. But what I'd like to know is, how did you change for the better because of it?"

She seemed stumped. Apparently, she had been so involved in the story that she hadn't taken time to see how the incident, whether real or perceived, might have impacted her in a positive way.

Her husband answered for her. "It gave her something to talk about besides my faults."

The room filled with laughter, and a man who had been taking copious notes dropped his pencil, grinning as he chased it down the aisle. Carl and Lydia had been sitting with frowns on their faces and now relaxed as the atmosphere lightened. A few more people asked questions, and I was able to reply without creating too much controversy. An hour later, I called for the last query.

The man who had dropped his pencil raised his hand. "Ms. Michaels, can you predict the future?"

"I can't tell you what you'll be doing a year from now, because you have the power to change things. However, if you continue to do and say and think the same things you have always done in the past, I can prophesy that the Law of Life will make sure you reap what you have sown, good or bad.

"I'm only presenting you with some new ideas," I said. "Hopefully, you will take them home, think about them, and then draw your own conclusions. I'm simply asking that you don't reject them at the outset. If, after truly examining what I say today, you think I'm full of it, that's perfectly okay. I'm only here to make you think. You have the power of choice."

CHAPTER FOURTEEN

REJECTION

WE FLEW HOME that evening, and sleep wasn't possible until after midnight. I woke the next morning to the shrill ring of the telephone and vowed I'd remember to turn off the ringer before going to bed again. I picked up the receiver and didn't even have a chance to say hello before Alex bombarded me.

"Mother, how could you? I mean, what did you say to those people? My friends have been calling me all morning wanting to know what's going on."

I rubbed the sleep from my eyes so I could attempt to comprehend what she was telling me. "What's this about, Alex?"

"Didn't you read the paper?"

My bedside clock read eight-fifteen. Normally, I would have had my breakfast and been finished with the L. A. Times by now. I usually skim the articles and avoid reading anything that contains violence in the headlines.

"You woke me from a sound sleep, sweetheart. Try starting at the beginning so I can catch on. What is in the news that has upset you and your friends?" I didn't even know her friends read newspapers. Ordinarily, they seemed too occupied with their own little worlds to worry about anything else.

"Just read page seven of the front section, Mother, and call me back."

She hung up on me. No sooner had I put the phone down, then it rang again. Robert didn't even attempt to hide his rage.

"What the hell, Paxton. Are you trying to ruin me? I've had three different clients call me this morning. Clients, Paxton. Not neighbors, not friends, but clients, whose business pays my bills. Yours, too, since you've insisted on spousal support."

He referred to the same page that Alex did. Since I had no idea what the article contained, I didn't defend myself, but said I'd call him back later. Angry now, I tossed the covers back, got out of bed, and stomped barefooted to the front door. The Times waited for me under the welcome mat. Before opening the paper, I made coffee. While the water ran through my Krups machine, I turned to page seven as instructed. Halfway down the page, I noted a short article with the heading *Local Woman Self-proclaimed Prophet.* I read with a grim foreboding.

On Friday, Paxton Michaels , wife of Beverly Hills businessman, Robert Michaels, spoke before a New Age group called The Millennium Society in Phoenix. Amid controversy, Michaels proclaimed herself to be a prophet, able to foretell the future.

The man with the pencil. He must have been a reporter. The article was only a few paragraphs long and focused only on the man's final question. He said nothing about the content of my talk or my responses to questions, and he deliberately misconstrued my meaning. No wonder my family was upset.

When I got Alex on the line again, I tried to explain what had happened.

"It doesn't matter how it went down, Mother. All my friends are laughing at me."

"They're not laughing at you, darling. They're making fun of something they know nothing about. If you explain to them that my words were taken out of context..."

"Do you really think they care? They're glad to have a reason to get on my case."

"Then they're not truly good friends."

"They're the only friends I've got," she whined. "Thank goodness I'm not going to school around here. Maybe by Christmas break they'll have forgotten about you."

Not if I continued to pursue my mission. I was sure the Martins would capitalize on the article to get me more speaking engagements. For a brief moment, I wondered if they had orchestrated the whole thing. Why else would a Times reporter be in Phoenix? Then I remembered that they hadn't been all that happy with some of my comments. All the way home they cautioned me not to be so controversial.

"Just tone it down," Carl had demanded.

I argued that new ideas were subject to disagreement more often than not, simply because they disputed thinking that had been in place and accepted for years.

Nothing I said to Alex made her feel better. I offered to invite her and her friends to my next talk so they could see first-hand that I wasn't a fortune teller, but she refused.

"No way, Mom." At least she stopped calling me Mother. She reserved that for the times when she hated me.

I didn't bother calling Robert. If Alex couldn't be convinced, no amount of argument would make my soon-to-be ex-husband see my side of the matter. Besides, I thought, he'd probably record the conversation and use it against me. A little voice in my head challenged me as I remembered my own admonition that beliefs create possibilities.

Moira and Jay showed up at two for a walk along the beach.

"Surprised?" Moira asked.

"Not really. I figure you came to talk about the article in the Times."

"You caught us," Jay said. "Actually, I wanted to hear your version. The reporter is obviously an ass. Maybe you should sue him."

"And be on the six o'clock news the minute the suit is filed? No thanks."

"Will this stop you from speaking in public again?"

I shook my head. "My dad used to quote something he found in an old autograph album. 'Whatever you are, be that. Whatever you say, be true. Straightforwardly act; be honest in fact. Be nobody else but you.' I guess I'm committed to what I'm doing, at least to the point of feeling like I have to continue."

Moira and Jay looked at each other. Moira spoke for both of them. "We kind of thought that's what you'd say. So just know we're here for you when you need us."

The Martins were delighted with the publicity. Carl thought it was good for our cause. "We've had half-a-dozen requests from groups who want to hear you."

"People who want me to tell their future?" I said.

"No, no," he assured me. "These are legitimate organizations that are looking for dynamic speakers. One I think we should consider is a rally in Orange County. You'll be one of four presenters."

"Who are the other three?"

"At this point, I'm not sure, but the promoter has done other all day events with people like Deepak Chopra and Greg Braden."

I had heard of both these men and believed they were well-respected as authors and lecturers. Although I'd never heard either of them speak, I knew they were touted to be spiritual people with a good message. Appearing with the likes of them would tend to give me some credibility.

"Okay," I said. "If you can arrange it, I'll do it."

At last the Martins were earning their keep.

CHAPTER FIFTEEN

GROWING CROWDS

ALEX THREW HER arms around me and squeezed. "I'll miss you, Mom."

"I'll miss you more," I said. "I've seen you nearly every day of my life since the moment you were born. Having you gone from my sight for weeks, maybe even months, is something that will take getting used to."

I thought about friends whose kids went off to school, fell in love, and moved with their new interest across the country to a place where the parents seldom saw them. And when grandchildren came... Well, I didn't even want to think about that.

Alex must have seen the tears in my eyes. "For heaven's sake, Mother, I'm only going to Berkeley. That's a five or six hour drive. You can fly there in forty-five minutes."

"I know, I know. It's just that you're growing up. Remember, though, you'll always be my little girl."

She rolled her eyes. "I'm a woman, Mother!"

"Barely." I placed one hand on a hip and shook a finger at her. "You wait, Alex Michaels. One of these days you'll be saying goodbye to your own daughter, and you'll understand then."

A sudden realization struck me. Even though I had been living alone for several months, Alex was never more than a few miles away. She often drove to the beach house to have breakfast with me, sometimes bringing friends and spending the day—at least, she did until my Phoenix trip. I never *felt* alone. Now, I'd be a victim of the empty nest syndrome.

The little voice in my head that I had come to recognize as David's said, *"Only those who believe they are victims are truly victims."*

I silently told David to shut up while I gave Alex a final hug and playfully pushed her toward Robert's car. He had agreed to drive her and her myriad suitcases and boxes to Berkeley in his new Lexus van. Apparently, the alimony he paid me hadn't drained his bank account too much. I blew her a kiss and waved as they backed out onto Highway One, heading north.

Without the distraction of helping Alex shop for school clothes, I could now concentrate on what I wanted to say at my next public appearance. Lydia had called that morning to tell me the date was firm. Advertising would begin immediately. I asked to see the contract.

"Of course, Paxton. I'll put a copy in the mail to you this afternoon. It's pretty straight forward. The promoter has agreed to pay us a percentage of the proceeds."

"I'm not sure I like the idea of being paid to speak."

"Don't be silly. Of course, you should be paid, just like the others on the program. It's not like you are charging the public directly. This man has put together a program to enlighten hundreds of people. Maybe thousands. The

Convention Center holds a heck of a lot of seats. He has to pay his expenses just like we do."

"Remember what I said, Lydia. I'm not doing this to become a millionaire."

She laughed. "No chance of that. We'll have plenty of expenses to cover ourselves—our own personal advertising, direct mail costs to our extensive client list, hotel and meals for the three of us. If it will make you feel better, we'll simply open an account in your name, maybe in trust for your daughter. Anything we make over and above expenses and our percentage as your agents will go directly to the bank. You never have to see it, and Alex will be pleasantly surprised when she graduates to find a little nest egg for the future."

I liked the idea. Between Robert's support checks and the settlement we had agreed on, I really didn't have to work. Having Alex benefit from what I was doing made sense. "That sounds great. Do it. Just give me a periodic accounting, okay?"

"That goes without saying. But don't be surprised if you don't strike gold. We're just beginning here, and who knows where it will lead? Maybe nowhere."

"I understand."

Lydia said she'd send me a signature card and asked me for a hundred dollars to open the account. "I think that's the minimum they'll take."

Apparently, my first speaking engagement hadn't resulted in a profit. I put the check in the mail.

September came and went. I spoke for several small groups locally and wrote a few articles at Carl's insistence. He made sure they got published in newspapers across the country with the intent of generating interest for a quarterly newsletter. I loved writing, and when I wrote about the First

Lesson, my pen flowed freely. The thought of sending out a written piece every three months excited me. It would be a wonderful way to give the idea to people without them having to pay to hear me speak.

Early in October, I began to have doubts about my ability to get up in front of three or four thousand people and carry on for an hour or more. I had plenty to say, but holding an audience that long would be difficult. I wasn't a professional speaker. Nevertheless, the day came when I climbed into the back seat of Moira and Jay's Cadillac and headed for Orange County.

We pulled up in front of the Disneyland Hotel at noon, just in time for lunch. I planned to eat lightly, spend an hour getting a massage, and then check out the facilities at the Convention Center with Carl and Lydia. The Martins didn't want anything to hold us up the next day. We needed to know where everything was, from our preferred parking to the ladies' room behind the stage.

"It won't look good if we're late," Carl said.

I agreed, not because I worried about appearances, but because, lately, I was compulsive about being on time for anything. If I intended to live with integrity, I needed to respect other people's schedules.

Once again, I asked the Martins about the contract for the event.

"I swear I sent it to you, Paxton," Lydia said, "when you first asked for it. I even tried to fax it to you, but your line always seemed to be busy."

"I've had a lot of trouble with that old fax machine," I admitted. "I really need to get a new one. Did you bring a copy with you today?"

"Gosh, sweetie, no. But don't worry your pretty little head about it. Carl and I have ironed everything out. Believe me, it'll go smooth as glass tomorrow. You'll see."

Lydia looked tired. Dark circles ringed her eyes, although she had diminished their appearance with skillful makeup techniques. I supposed she had been working hard on bringing this thing together. Besides, I had to trust them. They knew a lot more about these events than I did.

"I can't wait to see the bios on the other three speakers. I've never heard of them." The ridiculousness of that statement hit me. "But then, I suppose they've never heard of me, either."

Moira and Jay joined me for dinner. We snuck out of the hotel without telling the Martins, for fear they'd want to come with us. This would be the first time my friends had heard me tell my story to a crowd, and my nerves were on edge.

"You'll be fine, Paxton," Moira said, patting my arm.

"We'll be in the front row cheering you on," Jay assured me.

"With signs that say, *You Go Girl!*" Moira added.

"Oh, that'll do the trick, I'm sure." My mood didn't stay light for long. "Seriously, how do you think I'll compare to those other speakers? Carl tells me they're pretty well known."

"Not too well," Jay said. "I've never heard of them."

Moira lifted an eyebrow at her husband. "You don't run with their crowd, love. They're likely to have some pretty abstract things to say." She turned to me. "If it can't be proven scientifically, Jay isn't going to believe it."

"What happened to me can't be proven scientifically. Sometimes, I even doubt it. It all seemed so long ago."

"You're different. Jay believes everything you say."

Jay nodded. "I've never known you to lie or make up stories, Paxton. If you say it happened, it happened. If you say life is glorious, then life is fantastic."

I sighed. "We'll see if you still think that way tomorrow."

CHAPTER SIXTEEN

DAY OF ENLIGHTENMENT

"WE HAVE SEATS reserved in the first row," Carl said. "That way you can hear the other speakers." He repeated what I already knew. "You're third on the program, right after the lunch break."

"I doubt that I'll be able to eat. My stomach is already doing flip flops."

He gave me his standard pat on the knee. "You'll be fine. This crowd will love you."

I looked around for Moira and Jay, but the auditorium was rapidly filling, and it seemed impossible that I would be able to spot them. If only I had instructed Moira to wear a red hat or something. When I asked Carl if they could sit with me, he pointed out that the entire front row was taken up by speakers, presenters and those on the promotion team. This apparently included the Martins.

Glancing at the program, I noted that the other speakers had impressive credentials. Jim Gresham was president of the New Thought Alliance and pastor of the Healing Arts Society in Chicago. Belle Bottoms (surely that couldn't be her real name) had three master's degrees and had written seven books on near-death experiences. I hoped she wouldn't want to interview me for her next book, mistaking my experience as 'near death'. The final lecture of the day would be presented by John H. Banuelos. He, too, was an author. His self-help books, the program read, had been published in twelve languages, and he had lectured all over the world.

Carl pointed out that all three had tape series for sale during the breaks and after the program. He suggested that we should seriously think about doing something like this. It sounded awfully commercial.

A five-piece band played loudly for about thirty minutes while the seats filled with people. Finally, a buxom blonde in a navy sheath and red and blue paisley jacket walked up to the microphone and blew into it. Then she tapped on the instrument, creating a shriek of sound. That got people's attention. She waited for the crowd to quiet.

"Ladies and gentlemen! Welcome to this Day of Enlightenment. Prepare to be healed of whatever ails you."

That scared me. Carl and Lydia had persuaded me to talk about healing that day, something which David had touched on in our talks. Nevertheless, I felt as though he had barely scratched the surface of the subject, and wondered just how qualified I was to discuss it. I caved in to their demands; they convinced me how important it was to so many.

Both speakers that morning *were* enlightening. Gresham could have been a student of David's, and it felt wonderful to think I wasn't alone. He talked about the New Thought Alliance and how members of Unity, Religious Science, and independent 'New Thought' churches gathered together to support a fresh way of thinking about their spirituality. I vowed to seek out a local chapter. What impressed me most was how people in the audience reacted. Their faces held eager looks, and they applauded in agreement at the things he said. For a moment, I looked forward to my turn on stage. Then my nerves got the best of me again.

Belle Bottoms started out by saying that, yes, this was her real name. Her mother had been a hippie and a friend of musician, Frank Zappa, who had named his daughter Moon Unit. Belle's interest in near-death experiences began when she nearly died at the age of eight during an emergency appendectomy. She said she found herself hovering near the ceiling of the operating room watching the entire procedure. When the anesthesiologist urgently informed the surgeon that he was losing her, she felt like she was whisked away down a dark tunnel towards a bright light. Before she reached it, a voice urged her to go back, and she experienced a deep sense of regret at having to return to her body. That part felt quite familiar.

For years, she kept the event to herself, sensing that her stoical father would punish her for speaking such lunacy. As a teen, she chanced upon a book that talked of others who had had similar journeys, and the investigation of this phenomenon became her life's work. It wasn't the incident itself that seemed important to the people she interviewed; rather, it was the way it drastically changed their views of life and death. She seemed to give hope to the audience that there is truly something beyond our existence on earth, and that it matters how we conduct our lives. Once again, I thought she could have been the student of an angel at some time.

Throughout each presentation, a young woman stood at the side of the stage, translating the speaker's words into sign language for the hearing-impaired in the audience. Her hands moved fluidly, and it was difficult to take my eyes off her graceful motion.

I wandered through various exhibitor booths during the lunch break, hoping my jitters would disappear if my mind focused on something else.

Apparently, there was a big market for metaphysical merchandise. Bearded men and long haired women dressed like they might have grown up with Belle Bottoms' mother sold everything from massage devices to relax you into a meditative state, to candles, crystals, aromatherapy oils, New Age CDs and tapes, and books. A young man thrust a plastic bag full of brochures into my hand and a copy of the New Life Times. Another handed me a flyer about Tarot reading classes, and a girl barely out of her teens offered to tell my fortune for only a dollar a minute. I felt confused by the vast difference between the quality of what the speakers had to offer and the obvious commercialism of these other folks.

I allowed myself to be drawn into a small crowd that was listening to a tall native-American in full battle dress talk about finding peace within your own heart. His assistant handed out pamphlets which offered, for a mere $150, a session with this self-proclaimed medicine man that guaranteed to create prosperity in my life. I suspected it was designed to create abundance in the Indian's life, instead.

In my mind, I pooh-poohed the majority of the offerings, until I remembered something David had stressed. *A person is healed at the point he believes he is healed.* If people believed in these things, they might certainly create the desired effect in their lives.

I looked up to see Carl waving frantically to me. It was time to go back into the auditorium. Lights flashed on and off overhead, calling the audience to the next segment of the program. I had a sudden impulse to run the other way, but Carl reached my side before I could act on it. He took me by the elbow and prodded me toward the auditorium.

We returned to our seats just as my introduction started. I closed my eyes and mentally asked David to see me through this ordeal. *Don't worry, Paxton,* I heard. *What you need will be there when you need it.* Taking him at his word, I smiled when the applause began and climbed the stairs onto the stage.

CHAPTER SEVENTEEN

SURPRISES

THE APPLAUSE DIED down. I took a deep breath and dived in, beginning as always with the story of my accident and its aftermath. Because of the stage lighting, I couldn't judge the reaction of people beyond the fourth row. A few of the faces I could see registered disbelief, but others nodded knowingly as if they had been there alongside of me while I learned from David. The latter were in the majority, and I felt encouraged.

"David told me many truths, one of which is that we were all born perfect." I immediately detected a closing down of the openness in my audience. I shaded my eyes and squinted, trying to look beyond the first few rows. "I sense some disagreement out there. I had a great deal of difficulty with that concept myself and couldn't reconcile the idea with what seemed real. What felt real was my imperfection. Like you, I get sick and angry and resentful. Occasionally, I run red lights and get parking tickets. I gain weight at the drop of a hat. There seems to be nothing perfect about me. My daughter, Alex, was born six weeks early and had difficulty breathing on her own for a while. What could possibly be perfect about that?

"David assured me that the idea that created me is perfect, but in the physical world I live in, perfection is a potential I may never reach. The same holds true for each of you. You live within your apparent imperfection but, at the same time, you can recognize all of the ingredients for happiness that lie within it.

"That's where choice comes in. You can choose to be happy even when your world is collapsing around you."

At that moment, I realized just how true that was. Despite the devastation of losing my husband, my home, my way of existing for the past seventeen years, I actually felt content with life. My happiness no longer depended on what lay outside of me, but was totally based on what I thought about myself. I related this to the crowd and received scattered applause.

"What is perfection, anyway? Society's idea might be different from yours or mine. You might see that I don't drive a BMW or weigh in at 110 pounds, and I don't have a book on the best seller list or even a set of CDs to offer like the other speakers. Nevertheless, I assure you that I'm right where I need to be, doing exactly what needs to be done at this particular point in time. In my judgment, my life is perfect."

I changed gears a bit and focused back on my audience. "I suspect most of you are here today because you are seeking something. Maybe you think you want a better life, improved relationships, more money, or success? I believe that when we pursue the things that fulfill us and give us a sense of purpose, we are actually looking for ourselves. We have a natural instinct which tells us that we are continually becoming. Not becoming *something*, but simply becoming. At the same time, we have to remember that we are already *being*. It is in the day-to-day events that fill our lives that we must learn to make good choices for ourselves—choices that lead us to accept the idea of our perfection.

"Each of you made a decision to come here today, possibly because you merely wanted to learn something about yourself. Then again, it may be because there is an area in your life that needs to be healed.

"And that leads to the subject I want to cover today. Healing. It sounds implausible, but David says that anything can be healed—anything—if you choose to believe it can be done. He swears that damaged spinal cords can be made whole again and that missing limbs can be re-grown. Personally, I can't fathom this happening, so that kind of healing probably would not be available to me, regardless of what he says. But I can believe in simpler things. If I get a paper cut, I don't even think about it beyond the fact that it hurts for a short time. I know it will heal, and it does. The thing that heals that paper cut can also get rid of a tumor. It doesn't know the difference between big and small. If we choose to allow the process of healing to occur, it will.

"The unfortunate truth, however, is that when we receive a diagnosis of something 'big', like cancer, we focus on the cancer and its growth and negate the knowing that leads to healing.

Silently, I begged David to put the right words in my mouth that would help me convince people of the possibility of their own wholeness. It occurred to me that this might be the most important thing I could do with what I had learned from the angel.

"What is the difference between a paper cut or a cold or cancer? Or AIDS? What makes one seem so easy to heal and the other nearly impossible? Why does one seem small and insignificant and the other overwhelming? If you peer through binoculars, the objects in view appear to be larger. If you turn the binoculars and look through them the other way, objects appear to be smaller. The object itself hasn't changed, but your perception of it has! And your perception is where healing begins.

"It's time to remove the idea of big and little from your vocabulary. There are no big problems; there is only a belief in big problems. Change your way of looking at things and the solution is as near as your acceptance of it."

I had a lot more to say, and did. By the time the green light on my side of the lectern turned to red, my throat was dry, and I needed a drink of water. I concluded by assuring the audience they could cure anything if their belief in their own power was strong enough.

The mixed reaction of my listeners stunned me. When I finished, some folks stood and applauded. Others sat with their arms crossed. I had been sure, based on how they had reacted to the other lecturers, there would be a greater acceptance. The main difference in our talks, beside the fact that I professed to have a personal relationship with an angel, was the fact that I placed total responsibility for their lives on themselves. I guess that would be scary for some and instill guilt in others. I had gone through fear and blame, myself, after David explained my part in choosing my life's path. It's easy to take credit for the good things, but hard to accept that the bad is my doing, too.

I started to leave the stage when I noticed a woman struggling up the stairs on crutches. A man in the first row jumped up to help her. She hobbled toward me.

"Help me!" she shouted and reached out with one arm. "Please!"

I rushed to her, thinking she was about to fall. I grasped her hand and elbow. "What's the matter? Are you all right?"

She held my hand tightly and began to cry. The emcee thrust a microphone between us.

"I had an accident, too," the woman said. "Seven years ago. I've been unable to walk without crutches ever since. My doctors say I'll never be normal again, but I want to be well."

She sank to her knees, pulling me with her until we were both kneeling.

"You can heal me! I know it!" She hung on to my hand, pressing it against her chest. "Touch me. Make me whole again."

I tried to pull away, but she was strong. "I'm not..."

She swayed and fainted against me so that I had to hold on to keep her from falling flat on the floor. Before I could lay her down, her eyes flew open, and she jumped to her feet and began to dance.

"You did it! You did it! You healed me! I knew you could." She hugged me and kissed my cheek.

I shook my head. "No, no. It wasn't me. If you're well, it was you who did it. Not me. Not me."

The crowd was on its feet, shouting and clapping. I looked out and noticed only one person sitting in the front row, writing furiously on his pad of paper. It was the reporter from Phoenix.

CHAPTER EIGHTEEN

DENIAL

PANDEMONIUM ROCKED THE room. People stood, clapping, shouting, stomping their feet. Apparently, this was the kind of thing they had come to see. I shrank against the curtain behind me, while the woman waved her crutches over her head and walked back and forth in triumph. The only person frowning was the next speaker. It would be a while before the crowd quieted down to listen.

Moira and Jay fought their way through the throng along the middle aisle and onto the stage. Jay parted the curtain and peered through the opening. He beckoned to us. Moira put an arm around me and pushed me gently away from the noise and lights. Once out of sight, they prodded me into a fast walk. No one said a word until we were safely out of the building and hurried across the parking lot to Jay's car. I thought we had made it to safety without anyone knowing. I was wrong.

While Jay fumbled with the keys, I heard running steps approaching. "Ms. Michaels! Wait! My name's Fred Branstein. I'd like to ask you a few questions."

I knew before I turned that the reporter had followed us. Jay moved between the man and me. "She has nothing to say."

"Oh, come on. This is a chance for free publicity. That's what you're after, isn't it?"

Jay tried to shush me, but my retort fell out of my mouth like a kid on a slide. I couldn't have stopped it if I tried. "That's not what I want! I don't even believe what happened in there myself. I'm not a healer. I'm supposed to be a teacher."

Branstein cocked his head. "Supposed to be?"

I felt confused. "David—my angel..."

Jay interrupted. "I said she doesn't want to answer any questions. Now beat it."

His attempt to protect me calmed me down. "That's okay, Jay. Look, Mr....."

"Branstein."

"Mr. Branstein. Right now, I'm not sure what's going on. Maybe what happened in there was the next step in my mission. And maybe it wasn't. I just don't know. But if you'll give me your card, I'll call you after I have a chance to think this through and grant you an interview. But when I do, I'll want your assurance that you won't quote me out of context, and you'll let me see what you write before it's published."

His hesitancy was obvious. It took a minute, but he finally nodded. "I can live with that."

"She'll want it in writing, buddy," Jay said.

"She'll get it."

I reached out and shook the reporter's hand, thinking how much I needed him on my side. Moira nudged me, and I got into the back seat of the car. Moira joined me there, leaving Jay to act as chauffeur. We pulled out of the parking space and headed toward the exit. Luckily, we had checked out of the hotel earlier, and our luggage was stashed in the trunk. When we were finally on the freeway, I broke the silence.

"Strange, isn't it? No one followed us except the reporter. Not even the Martins."

"It was pandemonium in there," Moira said, reflecting my earlier observation. "They probably didn't even realize you had left. Every eye was on that woman prancing around the stage."

"You don't think I really healed her, do you?"

Moira looked at me and clucked her tongue. "I don't know, sweetie. You've gotta admit, it looked real."

Jay added his two-cents. "It looked damned phony to me."

I jumped at his angry tone.

"Sorry, honey. I'm as confused as you are. Real or not, the important thing is, everyone there seemed to think it was. They *wanted* to believe it."

I nodded. "David says it's what we believe about a thing that's important."

We drove in silence again for a while. I had an intense desire to be someplace else—any place but here in southern California on the Santa Ana Freeway. That thought triggered a memory. David had told me, *Everything is done according to one's preference.* When he instructed me to imagine myself in another place, I had opened my eyes to discover I was actually there. Would that work in this dimension? I decided to try.

I closed my eyes and imagined myself walking along a country road. Simply-dressed men toiled in the fields I passed, using horses to pull their plows, while women walked behind them, spreading seeds. They waved at me or, if they were close enough, greeted me with a pleasant, "Good morning." All seemed to take it for granted I belonged there.

I came to a group of houses clustered around a church and a one-room school. The roads were unpaved, and the thing that amazed me the most was the fact that there wasn't a car in sight. I had imagined myself into an Amish community.

A woman came out of one of the houses, wiping her hands on her apron. She waved and beckoned for me to join her on the porch. A pretty little girl brought a pitcher of lemonade and two glasses from the house and set them on the broad banister.

"You must be hot and tired," the woman said. "Let me pour you a cool drink."

I thanked her and sat on a bench to sip the tart, sweet liquid. It may have been happening in my imagination, but I could taste the lemon and feel the ice clink against my teeth when I up-ended the glass.

"Have you come a long way?" my hostess asked.

"A very long way," I answered.

"And have you far to go?"

"Much farther than I ever dreamed I'd be traveling."

"Has your journey taught you anything about life?"

"I've learned that life is full of surprises, and that, when serendipitous events occur, I must look at them as gifts."

"Then you have learned what you needed to learn up to this point in your travels." She stood, took the empty glass from my hand, and smiled. "Go with God."

With that, she disappeared into the house, her little daughter trailing along behind her. The girl turned before closing the screen door and winked.

From a distance, I heard a voice. "Paxton, wake up."

I opened my eyes.

"We're almost home," Moira said. "I was getting worried about you. I tried to wake you, but you were a million miles away."

I laughed. "Not quite a million, but far enough."

The phone was ringing when we entered the house.

"Don't answer it," Jay said. "Probably reporters."

"I have to. It might be Alex."

"Then let the machine screen the call first. If you want to talk to the caller, you can. If not, then don't."

I shrugged. Jay's ideas always sounded logical. We listened, together.

"Paxton, it's Lydia. If you're there, please pick up." She paused, waiting. I decided she could wait until tomorrow. "Well, call me when you get home. This has been the most exciting day! After you left, the crowd went wild, calling for your return. It took them a while to quiet down, and Mr. Banuelos was furious. He's a good speaker, though, so he had them eating out of his hand by the time he finished. But what I want to talk to you about is this wonderful healing power you've acquired. We can really make it work for you." Again, she said, "Call me the minute you get home."

"Oh, Lordy, that's just what I need. Someone like the Martins telling the world I have this power to make everybody well." I turned to Jay. "Don't let them do this to me."

"You don't have to do anything you don't want to do."

Moira looked thoughtful.

"What?" I asked, not sure I wanted to hear what she had to say.

"What if you really do have some tremendous gift? What if God wants you to share it?"

"In that case, I'll do whatever I'm directed to do. But things aren't always what they seem to be. She could have been a publicity seeker. Or maybe she was healed, but she's the only one I was supposed to touch? I still say that healing takes place because of one's own belief, not because someone laid their hands on a body part."

Jay took my hand and patted it, gently. "I agree that something doesn't seem kosher about this whole thing, and I intend to check it out if I can. But Moira's right. Most people can't heal themselves on their own. They need some symbol to let them know it's okay to get well. Maybe your hands are that symbol."

I held my hands up and examined them. Then I dropped them in my lap. In my heart, I felt sure. "No. That's not what I'm supposed to be doing."

CHAPTER NINETEEN

INTROSPECTION

THAT NIGHT, AS I often did, I sat on my deck listening to waves pound against the sand and communed with David.

"How can I be a spokesman for God when, sometimes, I don't even believe in God?" I said.

"Not at all?"

"Well, certainly not the God of my childhood. The idea of some guy with a long white beard sitting up in the sky in a place called Heaven, who metes out punishment and rewards, and who occasionally answers a prayer, seems absolutely ridiculous to me. Even the God you described as the One doesn't seem right to me most of the time."

David kept silent and listened.

"I think man invented God because of two—no, three things. One was a need to explain how the world was created long before we had any scientific knowledge.

"Secondly, out of desperation, people needed to explain why things happened; why children are born with six fingers instead of five; why a woman was attacked by a saber-toothed tiger; or why a lover walked out and chose another. We needed someone to blame. You know... 'It was God's will', and that sort of nonsense. Eventually, we gave him some help and thought up the devil."

David chuckled. *"Go on. I'm enjoying this."*

"Third reason: We needed some rules to live by, and what better way to lay down some rules than to have something or someone who has this humongous power tell us what we can and can't do."

I imagined David nodding his head in agreement, and argued further. "If there is a God, you can't even define Him. Anything you say is limiting. I heard someone use the term, Universal Intelligence, the other day. Even that isn't big enough to say what God is, because it only describes one aspect of him, or her, or it. And then there's the problem of which God is real. There are hundreds of religions, and only some of them believe in a Judeo-Christian deity. A few believe in many gods, not just one.

"I grew up as a Christian—at least, that's what my mom said I was—and I remember one of the Ten Commandments. Thou shalt have no other Gods before me. Then, a few centuries later, what did we do? We started worshipping Jesus. And some worship his mother. Even worse, I once knew a woman who told me, 'Paxton, every time I open up a door or go around a corner, I'm afraid I'll find Satan standing there.' She was so paranoid in her fear of the devil, that she gave him more power than she gave God."

I paused to see what kind of reaction I had gotten from David.

"My friend," he said, *"there is some truth in what you say, just as there is truth in every belief. No doctrine created by man, no definition of God, no idea of what God is or isn't, is totally true. Neither is any totally false. By its very nature, as you hinted, the One is too big to*

describe, too powerful to be contained in the box of definition. I don't blame you for not believing."

"But, David, I want to believe. Help me."

I pictured David looking up and stroking his chin while he thought. After a minute, he spoke. *"Do you believe in me?"*

"Well, of course."

"Why?"

"I've seen you, touched you."

"Have you? Or am I a dream that you had while you were in a coma?"

I laughed. "If you were a dream, I wouldn't be talking to you now, while I'm wide awake."

"Are you sure you're talking to me?"

Exasperated, I said, "Yes, David, I'm talking to you. I hear your every word."

He chuckled. *"With your ears?"*

"No, not exactly. I hear you inside my head."

"Inside your head," he repeated. *"Then how do you know I'm not simply a figment of your imagination, or like the voices heard by a schizophrenic?"*

I felt panic in my heart. "No, David, it's more than that. You're real. I know you are, because I can feel you. When you're around, I feel this overwhelming sense of love emanating from you."

Just then, the clouds parted and a full moon illuminated the sky above my house. It reflected on the rippling ocean and lit up the white caps that kissed the shore. There is a bacteria which creates a phenomenon that few are privileged to see. Where there was usually white foam on the waves pounding the beach, tonight, the foam was a brilliant, fluorescent blue.

"David, can you see that?"

"What are you feeling right now?"

My heart had filled up with what I can only describe as awe. "I feel... overflowing."

"Then perhaps that is how you can describe God. As a feeling, not as an entity. An overflowing of love."

I nodded my head up and down vigorously. "The few times I have been certain God exists, it is because I have felt something. A presence. A sense of wonder. A feeling of magnificent, awesome power, especially when I'm here at the edge of the ocean or standing in a grove of redwood trees. Like now."

David laughed out loud. *"So have we cleared up this little matter of not believing?"*

I laughed with him. "No. Yes. I guess I believe in something greater than I am, but I'll never be able to tell you what it is."

"Good enough."

Suddenly, David was gone. He often did this, coming when I needed to talk, leaving when he was satisfied that the need for talk was over. His satisfaction, not mine. I would have continued talking until daybreak if he would stay. There were always more questions. So many, perhaps they would never all be answered.

The next morning, I replayed David's words in my head. I had wanted to ask him about the woman who claimed she had been healed when I touched her and wished I had asked that first. Would I ever know what happened? Maybe Lydia and Carl could tell me.

It was nearly eight, time for my agents to be out of bed, I decided. My call was picked up by their answering machine.

"It's Paxton. Please call me as soon as you get this message," I said, and hung up feeling cheated. They probably had the ringer turned down low so they could sleep in. How dare they rest comfortably when I had tossed and turned all night long, my concerns repeating themselves in my head over and over, demanding answers, until I gnashed my teeth. Surely these two opportunists wouldn't have let a chance to pick up some publicity get away. They would have interrogated the woman, and now I wanted to grill them. I just hoped they hadn't contacted every newspaper, radio and TV station in the country.

In the meantime, cinnamon toast. My grandmother always cut it into four squares for me, and that's what I did now. Somehow it didn't taste the same if I left it whole. I pondered how *comfort food* could change the tone of a day, take me back to a time when I felt cared about and safe. I hadn't felt that way for a long time. For sure, the destruction of my marriage hadn't helped, and my newfound independence hadn't done much to make me feel good about myself.

Was this a *feel sorry for Paxton* kind of day, or was I being pressured by some inner urging to reach out and love someone who would love me back? I needed to hear Alex's voice.

When I called, Alex's breathless voice answered. “Hello.”

"Hi, honey," I said. "It's me."

"Mom! I was just talking about you. You remember Patti, don't you?"

I didn't, but she went on as though I did.

"Patti's mom is a channeler."

I'd never heard my kid sound so excited.

"Channeler? What's that?"

"She, like, goes into a trance, and then this entity from the planet Galblan speaks through her."

"Alex," I said, sounding more stern than I intended. "There is no planet Galblan."

"It's in another galaxy, Mom. You should hear this guy. He talks just like you."

I thought I understood. Whether Patti's mother was for real or not, Alex had found a common ground with her friend. She could talk about me and my experiences without fear, without feeling embarrassed to have a parent who had gone over the edge.

She didn't wait for my comments. "You've just gotta come up and meet Veronica."

"Patti's mother?"

"Yeah. She's way cool. Patti and I went to this occult shop where Veronica does her thing, and people were going crazy over her. She talks with an accent, sort of like she's from India or Pakistan, or maybe Russia. Her eyes are shut and she, like, looks really different when this guy starts talking. Except for the voice, he talks just like you, about being responsible for your own life and other weird stuff."

If he/she could get my teenage daughter excited about self-responsibility, this channeler might be well-worth meeting.

After I said goodbye, it occurred to me that this was the first conversation I'd had with Alex in over a year where we hadn't argued about something. Maybe more than one of us was changing.

I tried again to reach the Martins, but only talked to their message machine. Instinct told me they were doing their best to avoid me; but, for the life of me, I couldn't figure out why.

I decided that talking to Alex on the telephone wasn't enough. I needed to see her, put my arms around her and envelop my baby in a big hug. If I left now, I could be there in time for us to have a late dinner together.

"Can you be here before eight, Mom?" Alex asked when I called back and told her I was coming. "Veronica is doing a channeling session. I really want you to meet her."

"If I leave in the next ten minutes and don't stop, I can probably be there by six."

Having committed to that, I threw a few clothes in a bag and closed up the house. I pushed the speed limit to the max, knowing I could take a more leisurely route home. Even so, it was nearly seven when I entered the dorm. Alex sat in the living room, waiting.

"You're late," she accused. "Now, we'll only be able to hit Jack in the Box."

Old habits die hard, and I went on the defensive. "I drove as fast as I could without getting a ticket. Or worse," I said, remembering my accident. "I'm not ready for another hospital experience."

Guilt wasn't something Alex accepted, and she continued to grouse while I drove to the fast food restaurant. "I hate being late. You used to get me to school late all the time."

"That's not true, Alex. Oh, you were late a few times, but I always had you there by second bell." I refrained from mentioning that her tardiness had rarely been my fault.

"Yeah, right. No time to go to the restroom or say hi to my friends or cross-check my homework with someone. That's what I call late."

I wasn't going to win the argument, so I switched topics. "Tell me more about Victoria."

"Veronica," she said, correcting me. Baffled, I watched Alex glow with enthusiasm. "I'm really glad you're going to meet her. She's wonderful. Pretty, too. When she channels Maximus, her voice gets deep, and it doesn't sound like her at all."

"Maximus. Hmm, sounds Roman."

"Nope. He's definitely from another planet."

"In another galaxy."

Alex realized I was having fun with her and turned on me. "Yes, Mother. He's from another galaxy. Why does that seem so strange? After all, you talk to angels. Life on other planets sounds a lot more feasible than woo-woo spirits who live in the clouds."

She had me on the defensive again. I took a deep breath, relaxed my jaw which, by this time, had clenched so tightly I thought I might break a tooth. "David isn't woo-woo. And he *is* real!"

"Well, so's Maximus real. You'll see."

"Darling, let's not argue. Tell me why you think what Veronica or Maximus has to say is so profound."

I saw the tension in her shoulders let up. She didn't want to fight either.

"I'm not sure. Maybe it's because I can actually see Maximus when she goes under. Her whole body changes. She seems...." Alex searched for a word. "Bigger. Almost like she puffs up, like one of those blowfish, you know?"

I tried to understand. Seeing is believing. Funny, I think David would have said that believing is seeing. When you believe in something enough, it becomes visible in your experience.

"How many times have you seen her do her thing?"

"Only four. What I really want is a private session with Maximus. Veronica charges a hundred-fifty for an hour, but she said I could have one for seventy-five since I'm a friend of Patti's. Just imagine. A whole hour with him."

"And what sort of things would he tell you?"

"I don't know. Maybe, like, who I'm going to marry or something."

"A little soon to worry about that, kiddo."

She threw me a look of disgust. "I know that. But I'd like to have something solid in mind so that when he shows up, I'll recognize him."

"And lose the pleasure of getting to know him like other girls have to do? Be careful what you wish for."

Conversation stopped while we pulled into the drive-through and ordered cheeseburgers and Diet Cokes. We split an order of fries.

"Are you on a diet?"

Alex rolled her eyes at me. "Of course not. I just had three pieces of pizza while I was waiting for you."

At least some things hadn't changed.

CHAPTER TWENTY

MAXIMUS

WE ATE IN the car while I drove and got there ten minutes early. A crowd waited in line to hand over twenty dollars each to a young girl with six or seven earrings in each ear.

"Hi, Patti." Alex introduced me. "This is my mother."

Patti grinned at me and extended a hand, saying, "Hi, Mom." Her fingernails were painted black like her lipstick, and she had a frog tattooed between her thumb and forefinger. I wondered how long it would be before Alex followed suit.

"Glad to meet you, Patti." Was I really? I decided her impish grin was genuine, and it was impossible to dislike the girl. So far, at least.

"You're just in time. Veronica starts right on schedule so you'll have to wait until the break to check out her tapes and stuff."

The look on Alex's face said, "See? Late again."

I handed Patti a twenty. She took it, but kept her hand extended. "Oh, right. I forgot about Alex." I took another bill from my purse and put it into Patti's hand. Who would have paid for my daughter if I hadn't been there?

Even though the place was crowded, the front row held two empty seats. Alex maneuvered me towards them.

"I think I'd prefer to sit near the back."

"Oh, come on. I want you to see everything."

We sat in front. When we got comfortable, I casually mentioned that it seemed odd to hear Patti call her mother Veronica. "You're not going to start calling me Paxton, are you?"

"Don't be ridiculous, Mom. You and Veronica are way different. You'll see. Ssh, here she comes now."

I twisted my neck to find the woman Alex talked about, all the while wondering what, exactly, she meant by *way different*. At my first glimpse of Veronica, I understood. She was the most beautiful female I think I've ever seen. Long, coal black hair curled around her head. The fringe of lashes that shaded her chocolate eyes was so long they seemed artificial but, if they were, it was impossible to detect how they were attached. Alex was right. I couldn't deny that we were *way* different. I looked like a mom. Veronica looked like an exotic dancer. Long, lithe legs under her gauzy skirt guided her down the aisle. She had to be at least eight inches taller than I am.

"Isn't she gorgeous?" Alex asked.

I could only nod. Others in the audience, also seeing her for the first time, followed her advance to the stage with stunned gazes. She sat in a wide, throne-like easy chair and fastened a body mike to her low-cut blouse. Funny how the black dot of a mike can emphasize a well-tanned cleavage.

"Good evening, everyone. How wonderful to see you all here." She waved to Alex. "Hi, sweetie," she said, blowing her a kiss. "Maximus is eager to talk to all of you tonight."

She began by explaining what would happen. First, she would, through deep breathing, go into a trance. When she was fully under, Maximus would speak through her and give a fifteen minute talk on a subject he had chosen, and that it would be of importance to every person in attendance. Then, he would open up a dialogue with the audience. Veronica indicated a microphone standing in the middle aisle where people could ask questions.

"Are we ready?"

A murmur of agreement waved through the crowd.

Veronica crossed her legs in a lotus position and closed her eyes. I looked around, marveling at the rapt attention being given to this by the audience. Alex nudged me to concentrate on the stage. After a few minutes, Veronica began to twitch. She straightened in her chair and seemed to grow in stature. The illusion amazed me. Finally, with eyes still closed, she spoke in a heavily accented voice, deeper in tone than her own.

"Greetings my friends. We are Maximus and have come from a far distance to be with you tonight. There are those among you who are skeptical that we could travel so far in so short a time. When you are without form as we are, distance and time mean nothing.

"Although we are not aware of linear time as you know it, we must speak of it because it is important to you. The new millennium has leaped into existence in the midst of a great deal of fanfare and ceremony. You have acknowledged the accomplishments of the last thousand years and, particularly, have heralded the advancements made in the past century. Do you understand just how quickly things are moving forward? In the next hundred years, mankind will see even greater speed. Life itself is rushing through time. Cancer will be cured. AIDS will be eliminated."

Here she paused as if listening.

"Unfortunately, these diseases will be replaced by another, more devastating disease."

My first reaction was to disagree, but I could see where she was coming from. People don't seem to have reached the conclusion that it is acceptable to be healthy. When cholera could be stopped, tuberculosis became the thing to fight. When that was under control, polio became the pestilence of choice. When that could be prevented, the environment produced new cancers. When it looked like some forms of cancer could be cured, AIDS reared its ugly head. Now antibiotic resistant viruses are taking form.

I leaned over to whisper in Alex's ear. "Is she always this negative?"

Alex shushed me, and I returned my attention to Veronica/Maximus, who then answered my question.

"Always there is something to fight," Maximus continued, "something from which to die. When humans realize they are truly co-creating their world with God, they will turn to creating positive energy instead of negative. Until then, consciousness will continue to produce that which kills.

"Having said that, let us also say we are encouraged by men and women such as those gathered here this evening, who are learning the value of working together to create a more positive environment in which to live. You may recall that the Berlin wall fell shortly after people all over the world came together at the same time on New Year's Eve morning to pray for peace. You might say that their words had powerful wings, which beat down the wall of oppression, brick by brick, stone by stone, as its creators made the decision to join with the western world once again. World leaders may take credit for this, but we say to you that it was the common bond of intention that did it.

"Desire plus intent is the key to changing the world, just as it is the secret to changing your own lives. We long to remain youthful, but we must have the intention of being energetic, young at heart, alert, enthusiastic about life and creative, in order to be what we desire."

"Veronica must have met an angel, too," I whispered.

"Mother, don't be ridiculous."

I was taken aback by how condemning Alex sounded, but since two people shushed us, I didn't respond. I'm not sure I knew what to say to her, anyway, without sounding angry and retaliatory. I returned my attention to the speaker, but my concentration was broken.

A few minutes later, Maximus began taking questions from the audience. Most had to do with personal issues: 'When will I meet the man of my dreams?' or 'Should I get a new job?' The channel always turned the inquiries back to the people, somehow making sure they came up with their own solutions. I wasn't sure if this was proof that the answer to everything lies within or just good technique on Veronica's part.

When Maximus finished on stage, the crowd milled around, drinking hot cider and munching cold cookies, waiting for a chance to buy a tape of the evening's session. Veronica, herself, disappeared into a back room. When no more people stood at the money table, Patti shooed the last person out the door and locked it.

"C'mon, we'll get Veronica and split. How about fries and a shake at Bill Adams?"

"Is he a friend of yours?" I asked.

Patti and Alex practically rolled on the floor, laughing.

"No, Mom, Bill Adams is a place. A hang-out."

Feeling chastised, I grumbled, "Well, how was I to know?"

The giggling continued, like something hilarious had tickled their funny bone. I couldn't see the humor in it at all.

Veronica strode back into the room, having changed into a white, cotton pants outfit trimmed with fringe. Her hair was tied back in a pony tail, transforming her into a young girl instead of the forty-something woman I suspected she really was.

"Did I hear Bill Adams? Good. They have the best coffee on this side of town." She tossed her keys to Patti. "Here. You drive. I'm exhausted."

Alex looked at me, pointedly.

"You're not being subtle, honey." I handed my keys to her. "But I'm tired, too. I don't know if I'll get anywhere close to the witching hour. Don't forget, I still have to find a motel."

"Nonsense," Veronica said. "You'll stay with me. Come to think of it, why don't we let the girls go on by themselves. My brew is nearly as good as Bill Adams, and it only takes minutes to make a pot."

I didn't have to be convinced. Suddenly, I could hardly keep my eyes open. Veronica's offer sounded wonderful, and I told her so. I kissed Alex goodbye and said I'd take her to breakfast before getting back on the road for home in the morning. Alex reluctantly placed the car keys back in my hand, and the girls went on their way.

For all Veronica's flamboyance, her home was quite traditional. A two-bedroom cottage that may have reflected her financial status more than her style.

"Make yourself at home, Paxton. You can have Patti's room, the first door on the left down the hall, and she can sleep with me tonight. I'll have coffee ready in a couple of minutes, then we'll put some clean sheets on your bed, and you can conk out."

I dropped my overnight bag on the bedroom floor before joining my hostess in the kitchen. I sat at a butcher-block table and watched her work.

"It must be nice having Patti at home. I really miss Alex."

"Yes, it's nice. Most of the time. Sometimes I think it's better to have your child go away to school. I'm far too aware that my daughter's main objective is to develop an active social life."

She poured rich, dark liquid into a mug and placed it on the table before me, filled her own cup and sat down.

"Now, I don't have to be psychic to know that you have a lot of questions for me."

I shrugged, not knowing where to begin. "It's hard for me to believe that an entity from another galaxy can project himself light years from his home to speak through you at your beck and call."

She was silent for a moment, as if weighing how to answer me. "I know about your own experiences." When I gave her a surprised look, she said, "Alex told me. In light of that, I think I can be completely honest with you.

"I doubt very much that Maximus is what he says he is, even though it's an identity he insists upon. Because he reflects so many of my own beliefs, I tend to think he's actually a part of me. I suspect there's something deep in my subconscious that knows how to reach out and tap what might be termed the collective consciousness. Or maybe it's better known as the collective *un-conscious,* since it's beneath the surface. I'm not sure I'm making sense, because this is the first time I've put this into words."

Despite her speculation that Maximus wasn't an entity, I thought it was interesting that she still referred to him as *he.* Laughing to myself, I realized I had just done the same thing.

"So, do you think Maximus is something you made up?"

She thought about that seriously for a moment, then said, "Made up? Like is he just my imagination? No, I don't think so. He's taken on a life of his own in a way, sort of like when an author creates characters in a book and then doesn't have any control over what they do. They end up telling the story instead of the writer. And yet, they couldn't do it without the person doing the writing."

"Hmm, maybe he's the out-picturing of your own thoughts and beliefs."

She nodded. "If everything is energy as the scientists say, then even thoughts have intensity. Energy never dissipates. It just hangs around forever. Maybe even God's thoughts are wafting around the universe waiting for me to pick up on them."

Veronica's graceful hands lifted in a questioning attitude. "The truth is, I don't have any idea where the words come from. I only know that some of them are wise and, occasionally, I know things that I couldn't know by ordinary means."

I mulled this over for a few moments, amazed at how close she had come to reflecting my own point of view.

"Maybe there really is only one universal mind, and maybe we're all a part of it?" I said. "Perhaps that's why researchers on opposite sides of the world come up with the same conclusion or the same cure for a disease within days or hours of each other?"

Veronica placed her hand over mine. "I think there are many things we don't know."

I nodded. "Or will ever know."

We spent some time with our own thoughts, sipping our drinks. Finally, I had to ask the question that had been bothering me all day.

"Why do you think Alex can accept Maximus as being real, but gets angry when I speak of talking with an angel?"

My new friend gave me a sad smile. "You're her mother, and she only knows you as that. Remember, even Jesus had to leave home to perform his ministry."

CHAPTER TWENTY-ONE

SEARCHING FOR THE TRUTH

I TOOK MY time driving back to Los Angeles, cutting over to Highway One to enjoy the beauty of Big Sur. Later, in quaint little Cambria, I looked at store after store lined along the streets and thought they seemed to be lit from the inside out by dreams. Some would survive and others would fail. Was it purely a matter of choice? The owners had chosen their businesses, this neighborhood, a date to open. Could they choose to win or lose? Each one seemed alive with hope, but maybe the act of hoping was, in itself, a negative. At what point along the scale did hope for success become fear of failure?

By the time I pulled into my garage, it was nearly ten, and my eyes were ready to close. Two days on the road had gotten to me.

My answering machine blinked with more messages than I would have expected in such a short time, but I was too tired to listen to them. Once again, I played Scarlett O'Hara, and vowed to think about things tomorrow.

At six the next morning, I awoke to the jangling insistence of my telephone. Jay didn't even give me a chance to say, "Hello."

"Where have you been? I must have left you a dozen messages yesterday, and more the day before."

"Well, good morning to you, too. I drove up to see Alex." Offended by his attitude, I said, "I wasn't aware that I had to check in with you before I left town."

Jay laughed then. "Whoa, girl, I guess I did sound dictatorial. I apologize."

Satisfied, I accepted his repentance. "Now, what's up?"

"What's up, indeed? Your so-called agents are being sued by at least three different clients for mismanaging funds and numerous other misdeeds. I say three, but I've only checked Los Angeles County. There may be more."

"No!"

"Yes, ma'am. It was easy enough to check the public records. Seems they have a tendency to take in more money than they report to their clients."

"Oh, great. I've been asking for an accounting. They insist that because I won't let them charge people to hear me speak, the only thing we've done is cover travel expenses."

"Strange, isn't it, when they're supposedly operating on a percentage? What about Anaheim?"

"The promoters paid us a fee," I said.

"How much?"

I had to admit I didn't know.

"Well, I do," Jay said. "I made some inquiries."

"And?"

"A check was issued to you for $10,000."

"Ten thousand dollars!"

"You've got it, sweetkins."

"But that's ridiculous. I only spoke for an hour. Why haven't they been returning my calls? And where's my money?"

"Good question. Perhaps we should find out?"

It had been less than three days since the fiasco in Anaheim, and I hadn't listened to my messages. Maybe the Martins had phoned. I told Jay I'd call him back. As soon as I hung up, I played back my machine. Boyd Perkins, the actor who had shared Carl and Lydia as agents, left a cryptic message.

I've been on location, and will be back next week. If you're dealing with Carl Martin and his wife, we'd better talk.

A woman who said her name was Celia Brown called. *Mr. and Mrs. Martin gave me your number. I have to see you. Please call me.* Her area code indicated she lived in Los Angeles.

The rest of the messages were all from Jay. Messages about Lydia and Carl, but none from them. I dialed their number, hoping to get them out of bed. No luck. Their own message machine was turned on.

"Call me the minute you get this," I said. "If you don't, there will be hell to pay."

I was hopping mad. Not only had the Martins avoided me after my last speaking engagement, they had given my number to a stranger. I valued my privacy now that I had become a minor celebrity. How did the so-called stars do it? I guess they hired agents who took better care of them than the Martins did of me.

When I called Jay again to let him know I hadn't received word from them, he promised to expand his investigation. I vowed to do what I could from my end.

After a shower and a cup of coffee, I decided to call Celia Brown. The excitement in her voice when I identified myself was obvious.

"Oh, thank you for getting back to me. I saw you at the Convention Center. You healed that woman who came up on stage."

"Now, wait a minute," I said. "I'm not sure about that."

"Well, I am. You left the auditorium, but I stayed to talk with her. She said she had been crippled by an accident and had been walking on crutches ever since. The next step, her doctor told her, would be into a wheel chair. If only you had stayed to see how well she was after you touched her…"

"Celia, she may have been a plant. My agents aren't exactly trustworthy, and I'm afraid they might have hired her for a publicity stunt."

For a minute, I thought she had hung up, but she had just gotten quiet. When she spoke again, I heard disappointment in her voice.

"I see. Then you don't have healing powers."

"I don't know. That's as honest an answer as I can give you." I wondered why she needed to know. "Are you ill?"

"No," she said. "Not me. My little girl has leukemia. Tracey's only three. We haven't found a bone marrow donor to match. She may not live to see her fourth birthday."

Chills ran up my spine. I couldn't imagine the pain of knowing my child might die and there was nothing I could do about it.

"I'm sorry, Celia. I wish I could help."

She sounded hopeful. "Maybe that woman was telling the truth?"

I doubted it. If she had been, surely one of the Martins would have been bugging me.

"Will you do me a favor?" my caller asked. "Will you just see Tracey for a few minutes? Maybe lay your hands on her? Just to humor me, of course. I'm desperate."

Fear gripped my solar plexus. If I refused to see her and later found out I could have helped her… What if I was too late?

"All right. But I guarantee nothing."

The Browns and their little girl lived in a small, older cottage in the Silverlake area near Hollywood. I had a heck of a time finding a parking place. Evidently the homes in this neighborhood had few garages or multiple car owners, and I ended up parking nearly two blocks away. My trek on the badly repaired sidewalk was uphill, and I was grateful once again to Herman and his insistence that I keep up my therapeutic exercises beyond what the doctor ordered.

Although I'd used the excuse that it might be better for Tracey if I saw her in her own environment, the truth was, I didn't want word getting out about where I lived. My privacy was fast becoming a vital necessity for my own feeling of well-being.

The Browns' house was what my mother used to describe as neat as a pin, whatever that meant. Outside, the tiny plot of grass between the raised porch and the sidewalk was mowed and bordered with rose bushes. The steps were swept and the place looked freshly painted. I already had a good impression of Celia Brown.

My knock was answered in seconds. When she opened the door, Celia stepped out onto the porch and hugged me.

"Oh, I'm so glad you came. Thank you so much."

"It's my pleasure," I said. That wasn't quite a fib, because I was curious to find out if some sort of healing power actually existed in me.

The inside of her home was as neat and clean as the exterior, although it seemed obvious by the vintage of the furniture that nothing new had been purchased for years. Probably most of their funds went towards medical bills.

"My husband is at work," Celia said, "but he can come home if you'd like to meet him."

"I'm sure that's not necessary. I'm more interested in meeting Tracey right now."

"She's in the kitchen having some juice. Do you mind sitting there with her?"

"Of course not," I said. I waited for her to lead the way, but she stood in place, looking uncomfortable.

"Um, before we go in, there's something I guess we should discuss. We don't have much money, Ms. Michaels, but I can pay you in installments if that's okay with you."

"Pay me? Oh, Celia, I'm not going to charge you for this. I don't even know if it's going to work. And even if it does, I don't think it's right to make a fortune off of other people's troubles."

She burst into tears. "It's been so hard. Tracey's illness has drained our bank account. Richard, my husband, is working two jobs. You can't imagine how much her hospital stays are costing us, even with insurance."

I did know. Only I was lucky enough to have an insurance company pick up the entire tab. The other driver's carrier and father had been so grateful that I hadn't sued, they gladly paid all my bills and bought me another car.

I patted her shoulder. "Let's see what we can do. Introduce me to your daughter."

Celia led me to a small kitchen that had room at one end for a little table with three chairs crowded around it. In one of the chairs, sitting on a booster seat, a thin child sipped apple juice through a straw. I wanted to cry when she turned to me. Dark circles rimmed her brown eyes, making them appear too big for her diminutive face. Reddish-blonde fuzz covered her head instead of curls. Every movement seemed to be an effort.

"Honey, this is Ms. Michaels."

I sat down across from the girl. "You can call me Paxton, okay?"

"That's a pretty name," she said.

"So is Tracey. What's your middle name?"

"Elizabeth."

"Tracey Elizabeth Brown. That's lovely. Just like you," I said, and meant it. The effects of her illness couldn't hide the fact that she was a beautiful little girl. I engaged her in a little more small-talk, hoping to make her comfortable in my presence before trying to touch her. In a few minutes, I asked, "Would you like to sit on my lap?"

"Okay."

Celia lifted Tracey from her chair and placed her on my knees. I noticed that she winced when her mother picked her up.

"Does it hurt to be touched?"

Tracey nodded.

"I need to touch you a little bit, but I promise I'll be really careful. I don't want to hurt you."

Trusting eyes gazed into mine. "Okay," she said again.

Suddenly I realized I had no idea what I was doing. Mentally, I called for David. *What the heck do I do now?*

The answer came. *Do what feels right.*

What felt right was to place one hand on Tracey's back and one on her chest. I did that and closed my eyes, visualizing a white light coming from my hands. To my surprise, Tracey laughed.

"That tickles. And it feels warm."

Something was happening. I felt a tingling sensation in my palms, then a resistance, almost as if there was a magnetic force between them. It remained for two or three minutes, then diminished. I opened my eyes. Tracey slumped against me, her mouth forming a little "o" as she snored gently.

Tears streamed down Celia's cheeks. "She has such a difficult time sleeping. Even the pressure of blankets is hard for her to bear. If all you've done is help her to rest, I'll be grateful. But I hope there's more."

"So do I, Celia. So do I."

CHAPTER TWENTY-TWO

THE INTERVIEW

THANK GOODNESS THE walk to my car was downhill, for I felt exhausted. All I wanted to do was sleep, but I had a long drive ahead of me. My body won out. When I got behind the wheel, I put my head back and closed my eyes. Forty-five minutes later, someone tapped on my window.

An old man looked in. "You all right, lady?"

I rolled down the window. "Yes. Thank you for being concerned. I've been sleeping, but I'm fine now." And I was, even feeling rejuvenated. The drive home through the canyons reminded me just how beautiful the world can be. Sunlight and shadows played on green hills that would soon be turning brown for the winter, and I drove with the windows open, smelling a freshness that usually only came after a rain.

I'm not sure what happened with Tracey that day, but it affected me, as well. I felt better than I'd felt since before my accident. David's law of reciprocity that he had emphasized so strongly evidently worked. When you give, you receive in kind. I thought of the doctors and nurses I knew. Most of them were healthy and vibrant. They gave health. The most prosperous people I've met give large amounts of money to others. Kind folks are likely to receive gentle treatment in return.

My ex-husband was well-to-do, though, and he certainly wasn't a giver. He just expected to live well. So expectations must enter into the formula, too. Then I remembered that quite a bit of his income came to me each month. Being able to make money didn't always mean getting to keep it all. For just a moment, I felt sorry for him, knowing how much it must hurt him to write that check every thirty days.

I quickly moved my thoughts back to something more positive. Thinking back over the past few months, I realized how much good had come into my life. What had started out as a tragedy had turned into something far better than I could ever have imagined for myself. David had changed my thinking about how God existed as a part of my life. Robert's leaving had made me stand on my own two feet for the first time. Alex, who had been rebelling against both her dad and me, had begun to be my friend. Veronica treated me to a whole new concept of how knowledge and wisdom can present itself. In a brief conversation with Robert the day before, even he had commented on my new strength. For the most part, I liked this new me. And now, just maybe, I had become a hands-on healer. I wouldn't know for sure until Tracey proved me right or wrong; but oh, how I wanted to be right.

When I left the Brown's house, Tracey was still sleeping, and Celia looked like she could use some rest herself. She promised to call me if there were any changes in Tracey's condition.

My next task was to get to the bottom of whatever scheme Carl and Lydia Martin had cooked up to take advantage of the public—and me.

"Fred Branstein?" I said.

He had answered the phone with a disinterested, "Yeah." I could hear the chatter of his keyboard in the background.

"This is Paxton Michaels."

The typing stopped. "Paxton!" So, now we were on a first name basis. "I'd been having second thoughts about you. Didn't really think you'd call. It's great to hear your voice."

I got right to the point. "I think we should talk."

"Hey, I'm ready any time you are," he said. "The sooner the better."

"What about tomorrow morning?" I decided to take a big chance and give up my privacy. "You can come here."

"Your house? Wow, can I bring a photographer?"

"Absolutely not. This is between you and me. No one else, understand?"

"Sure, you can trust me."

Could I? If not, I might be putting my dream house on the market and moving to some remote corner of the world to get away from the publicity he could create. And yet, my instincts told me I was safe. If I gave this guy a really big story, he'd make sure to protect me from other reporters. He'd have an exclusive as long as he kept me isolated.

I gave him the address. "Be here at eight, and I'll have coffee made."

After leaving messages again for the Martins and Boyd Perkins, I set up my easel and began mixing colors. It had been a long time since I had painted, and the urge to create was too great to ignore. My favorite medium was watercolor, but this time I felt impelled to work in oils with a palette knife. Before long, the vivid hues of David's world sprang to life on my canvas. Would anyone believe that this world actually existed? I decided it didn't matter. It was real to me, and that's all that counted.

That night, exhausted from the day's activities, I slept like a baby, curled into a fetal position. I woke up in nearly the same spot as when I went to bed, feeling refreshed, with a vibrant suspicion that I had never been more alive. Is this what comes from taking charge of your own life?

Fred Branstein arrived at precisely eight o'clock. I watched him through a window, amused that he sat in his car for nearly fifteen minutes before getting out to knock on my door at the stroke of the hour. He must have learned that at some seminar.

"Come in, Mr. Branstein."

He followed me to the deck where I had set up the coffee pot.

"I hope it's not too cold for you out here," I said. "If it is, we can go inside."

I was dressed in sweats and a windbreaker to protect me from the brisk, ocean breeze. The sun wasn't high enough to bring much heat. The reporter had a light-weight sports coat over a short-sleeved cotton shirt; probably not enough to shield him from the morning chill.

"I'm fine," he said. I assumed he was probably lying when goose bumps appeared on his hairy wrists. Well, he was an adult and, if he wanted to go inside, he'd have to ask. Laughing to myself, I got a thrill out of my new-found power. If I could take charge of my own life, then so could he. In my head, I heard David signal, *Bravo!*

After Fred stirred three sugars and a dollop of cream into his mug, he pulled a pad of lined paper from his inside pocket and clicked his Bic pen open. I waited for his first question, although I planned to take control of the interview after his initial examination. He asked for the correct spelling of my name and permission to record the interview, which I agreed to if he would give me the same privilege. We both clicked on our recorders and set down the rules for our verbal exchange. I agreed to answer his questions as honestly as I could, and he agreed not to print anything without my okaying it first. Hopefully, he'd keep his promise.

"Before we begin, Mr. Branstein, let me ask you a question. Why have you been so interested in me? You followed me from Los Angeles to Phoenix to Anaheim and back."

He had the courtesy to look sheepish. "Frankly, I was hoping to expose you as a fake. Now, I'm not so sure you are."

That was a good answer. Did he say that to throw me off guard, or did he mean it? "Why was it so important that you expose me if I was a fraud?"

"My mother's sister was taken in by a religious cult—remember Jim Jones? Her beliefs cost Aunt . Jenny her life."

I shuddered. "I remember. He's the one that persuaded his followers to commit suicide with him. They took poison, right?"

He nodded, tears brimming his eyes.

"But I don't profess to be a religious leader. I haven't started a cult."

"By definition, a cult is simply a group of followers of a certain belief. A broader, looser definition, which is pretty much accepted, is any belief outside of so-called normal Christianity."

"Like the Mormons or Christian Science."

He squinted, considering this. "Technically, yes. But it's the Jones' group and others like them that cause problems." He smiled and shrugged. "When someone professes to talk to angels, it's like saying you've got a direct line to God. Whether you mean to start a new religion or not, it could happen. And if you didn't agree to be the leader, others could interpret what you say whatever way they want. Look at how St. Paul added all those rules and regulations to Jesus' words."

I had to laugh, but at the same time what he said worried me. Lydia and Carl Martin could be my Paul. "I think we're on the same track here, Mr. Branstein."

"Fred," he corrected me. "Do you mean with your agents?"

Surprised, I asked, "What makes you think that?"

"I've heard some things."

I waited.

"I've been doing some digging. It seems they have a long list of dissatisfied clients." He told me about the same lawsuits Jay had mentioned. "These are the ones that are pending. There have been others, but some were settled out of court, and they've actually won a few. Don't know how, but it would be easy enough to pull the paperwork."

He was pretty thorough. I'd have to get Jay a copy of my tape, although he'd probably kill me for doing the interview without him.

"How did you get involved with them in the first place, Paxton?"

I told him how they had contacted me and that I'd been searching for a way to tell my story. "I jumped at letting someone else do the planning and legwork."

"Since I had hoped to do an expose, maybe my piece will be more on them than you. Any objections?"

I shook my head. A thread of something had been running through my mind, and I wasn't sure I felt comfortable letting someone else write my story. I wanted to do it myself.

We spent the entire morning together and ended with ham and cheese sandwiches and a glass of wine. I felt like I'd made a new friend. Or, if not a friend, at least an ally.

That afternoon, Celia Brown called, sounding excited. "The most amazing thing has happened! Tracey's doctor called. They've found a bone marrow donor. She goes into the hospital on Tuesday. This is what I've been praying for. She's going to be all right now, I know it."

"That's wonderful news, Celia," I said.

It *is* great news, I told myself after we ended our conversation. I'm happy for Tracey and her family. In the back of my mind, however, was an ungenerous thought: *Now, I'll never know if I was able to heal her.*

CHAPTER TWENTY-THREE

TRUTH OR DARE

I WAS DEPRESSED despite being elated over Tracey's good news. It's funny how our perception of things affects our emotions. But then, David said that perception is everything. It creates our reality. Two people going through similar situations can have entirely different experiences.

The first time I had my own money to buy Christmas presents, I purchased a simulated pearl choker for my mother. When she opened her gift, she oohed and aahed appropriately, but then said, "Is that all you got me?" Today, I believe she meant to ask if there was another gift she should look for and open. Then, however, my little child's heart sank. In my youthful perspective, I hadn't given her enough. That event colored the way I experienced the holiday from then on. I over-spent for gifts in the mistaken hope that they would ensure the recipient's love for me. It wasn't until I met David that I realized how my own mind had created the stress that came with each December 25th and every family birthday. And what we create, we can re-create. This year, I'm painting everyone something special that reflects their taste, not mine. I'm giving them my love, rather than an expensive present.

I tried getting in touch with David to discuss my feelings about Tracey, but my angel was strangely silent. Once again, it seemed, I was on my own.

As the morning progressed, I learned more about Carl and Lydia, and I didn't like what I heard. Fred Branstein messengered over a summary of a court case in San Bernardino County where the Martins had been sued by an Olympic ice skater for misrepresentation. Apparently, the agents had a good lawyer, and only had to give up $10,000 to settle the case.

Jay told me he had sent an investigator to the Martins' office, and found a "For Lease" sign on the window.

Finally, Boyd Perkins phoned again.

"Ms. Michaels, I told you I'd call when I got back into town, but I had some free time today and decided not to wait. Our shoot shut down because of a rainstorm. We're doing exteriors, and the scene calls for blue skies. Besides, none of the crew wanted to brave a potential lightning strike."

"I'm grateful that you called, Mr. Perkins. I'm really eager to hear what you have to say about your former representatives."

He laughed. "Their main thrust, it seems, was to bankrupt my career. Oh, they got me a few acting gigs, all right, and they took the standard ten percent of what I made. But they also billed my employers for expensive perks that I never saw. Like champagne and fresh flowers in my dressing room and limo rides to and from the studio. Until recently, I was basically a nobody in the industry. How they talked the film execs into things, I'll never know. However, they are good at what they do when they want to be. If they were legitimate, they'd probably make a fortune. Anyway, they kept the bouquets and bubbly for themselves or produced false receipts and took the company's money. Because of them, I'd gotten a reputation of being a prima donna, if a guy can be that."

I wondered what David would say about Boyd's participation in the scam. If we create our own experience, he must have drawn it to himself somehow. I had no more than formed this idea when he confirmed it.

"When I was new in the industry, I was desperate for work. Not because I needed the money, necessarily. My parents were happy to subsidize me, but I wanted to be a star and didn't have the confidence that I'd make it. They sold me a bill of goods about how they could make me great, and I bought it. Didn't even check them out. They were the first agents who took a look at me. My resume had only one student film and a bit part in a high school stage production when I was seventeen. Not very impressive. I sent out pictures, but never followed up. I was offered a few things that didn't pay, but said I didn't work for free. A mistake, of course. Anything on my resume might have helped. When the Martins called, I'd all but given up hope that I'd ever get an agent.

"In all honesty," he continued, "they did get me work that I wouldn't have gotten otherwise. That's why I never went after them. And now I have a new manager. It's a lot easier to find a representative when you already have one."

"I understand the Martins got you the picture you're on now and that it's going to make a star out of you."

"It may make me a star, I don't know. But it wasn't them who got me the gig."

I shook my head, wondering how I could have been so naïve as to believe them. Now their lies were coming back to haunt them. I marveled that they might not even care.

We ended our conversation on a friendly note. He even said he'd send me an invitation to the film's premiere.

Apparently, Carl and Lydia did just enough good to get by. I wasn't sure how much good they had done for me.

Later that day, Moira showed up on my doorstep. "Get your bag, honey, you're comin' with me."

Grateful to get out of the house and do something besides brood over what the Martins had or hadn't done, I did as she said. It wasn't until we were zooming back towards Santa Monica on Highway One that I asked where we were going.

"Beautiful downtown Santa Ana. Jay found your runaway."

"Runaway? I'm confused."

"The woman you healed, silly. You and I are going to surprise her."

I buried my face in my hands. "Oh, God, Moira, I don't know if I'm ready for this. Does she know we're coming?"

"I told you it was a surprise. You've got to start listening better, kiddo. She works at McDonald's. Feel like a hamburger?"

"We're going to her workplace? Moira, she might get fired."

"Didn't you say we create our own experience? Well then, she can reap what she sowed."

I wanted very much to confront the woman and find out the truth, but I didn't want to hurt her in any way. "Promise you won't make a scene. We can wait 'til she takes a break or something."

Moira scoffed at the idea. "She didn't mind creating a scene the other day. Why change things now?"

"Moira! Stop it. I'm not out for revenge. Just a little knowledge about myself." Relenting, I patted her knee. "Besides, you can catch more flies with honey than with vinegar."

My friend pouted for a minute, but her natural, sunny countenance broke through the gloom and she gave me a bright smile. "Oh, all right. You've always been too tender-hearted for your own good, but I'll go along with it. Honey it shall be."

It took nearly two hours to get there. By that time, I really did want a hamburger and said so. "Fries, too. And maybe a milkshake."

"Honey bun, you're gonna get as big as a house. They have salads, too, you know."

"And I want cheese on my sandwich," I teased. "A double helping."

Moira grimaced. "Oh, my cholesterol. I feel it rising. I'm getting lightheaded. Oooh, my heart."

Sudden paranoia came over me. "Stop that right now! Your words have power. I don't want you getting sick."

Shocked, she said, "Hey, I was just kidding."

I calmed down a bit, but felt the need to lecture. "I know. I'm just so acutely aware that the seeds we plant can come to fruition if we keep fertilizing them with similar thoughts. One sentence isn't going to raise your cholesterol or cause a heart attack, unless you actually believe it. But if you continue to say things like that, your subconscious mind will latch onto it as something you really believe. Then watch out."

Moira fell silent as we pulled into the restaurant's parking lot. I felt like a mother scolding her child.

"I'm sorry," I said. "Please forgive me for railing at you."

She turned to me. "My doctor just put me on medication for elevated cholesterol."

We stared at each other for a full minute, then fell into a hug.

"Come on," she said, pulling away. "Let's find out if you have that healing power, so you can help me."

"Moira…"

"Shut up and get out of the car, cookie. I'm counting on you."

We hugged again before going inside.

I recognized the woman immediately. "There she is, wiping off that table. Do you know her name?"

Moira consulted a paper she pulled from her jacket pocket. "Beatrice Tremell. She has worked here a little over a month. Jay's investigator had a heck of a time finding her. I'm still not sure how he did it. Jay usually doesn't ask."

"Let's get our food first and watch her for a while. I don't see evidence of any crutches."

"No, and the private eye said she never brought them to work, either. As far as anyone here knows, she's fit as a fiddle and passed her medical exam with ease when she started working."

We ordered our food. I did get a cheeseburger and fries, but opted for iced tea instead of a milkshake. Moira had a salad with chicken and squeezed lemon on it instead of the ranch dressing she loves.

Our quarry seemed to be a good worker. The minute someone rose from a seat, she had her cleaning rag ready. Twice she ran after folks who had left something behind.

"At least she's not a thief," I said.

We nursed our coffees until Beatrice took a break. She sat at a corner booth with a dish of soft ice cream and a soda.

I watched her slip off her loafers and rub her tired feet. We walked over to her and slipped into the booth, Moira on Bea's side, and me sitting across.

Beatrice looked startled. "Hey, this is my booth. Do you mind?" She looked around. "There's an empty one there." She pointed to the place we had just vacated. Then she looked at me and squinted. "Oh, Lord. It's you. How did you find me?"

Moira started to speak, but I held up my hand. "It doesn't matter how we found you, Beatrice. We just want to talk for a few minutes. You're not in trouble, and we won't jeopardize your job."

She relaxed only slightly and wore a cornered animal look on her face.

"All I'm interested in is Carl and Lydia Martin's role in what happened in Anaheim a few days ago. What they told you and what they asked you to do." I leaned forward, speaking confidentially. At least hoped I came across that way. "You weren't really crippled were you?"

Her face crumpled and I thought she was going to cry. "N-no. They told me to say I had been in a bad accident, but I hadn't. The crutches were brand new, from them."

"Did they pay you to say you were healed?"

"Yes ma'am. Two hundred dollars."

My heart sank. I hadn't realized how much I was hoping to hear that God was using me as a vehicle for healing. Suddenly, I couldn't think of another thing to ask. I had gotten what I came for, and I didn't like it one bit. I stood up and slung my purse over my shoulder.

"Thank you, Beatrice. You've been quite helpful. Come on, Moira."

My friend fished a card out of her purse. "Here's my husband's number, Beatrice. If you think of anything else we might need to know, call him."

I led the way outside and waited for Moira to unlock the car. As we pulled out of our parking place, Beatrice tapped on my window and motioned for me to roll it open.

"Miss Michaels, I don't want you to think I'm a bad person. I really listened to what you had to say that day, and I'm trying to use it. It's hard, though. My pastor says everything's God's will, even the bad stuff. But when I look at what's happened to me, I can see how I created a lot of it myself. You keep talking to people, okay? Maybe more of them will learn something like I did."

"Thank you, Beatrice."

"You can call me Bea," she said with a tentative smile.

I smiled back. She wasn't such a bad person. "And you can call me Paxton." I started to roll up the window.

"Wait! One more thing," she said. "My blood pressure's been high—about 160 over 95. When you grabbed me, trying to keep me from falling down that day, I felt an electric shock. I just thought you should know. I went to the doctor yesterday, and my pressure's down to 130 over 80."

CHAPTER TWENTY-FOUR

THINGS ACCELERATE

ON THE WAY home, Moira and I argued. "It could be a coincidence," I insisted.

"It could be that you really helped her."

"Come on, Moira, haven't you gone to the doctor and had your blood pressure checked and found it was way up or way down depending on how much stress you had in your life? That woman might have had financial problems and the money Carl paid her relieved a lot of that stress."

Moira snorted. "Two hundred dollars? That buys her a couple of dinners out and a pair of stockings. What kind of relief does two hundred dollars get you?"

"Well, we don't know what else might be going on in her life. Maybe it was just enough to pay off an old gambling debt. Or something." Even to me, that sounded pretty lame. We both started to laugh at the same time. "Okay, okay. I'll concede that *maybe* there's something to it, but how in the world can I prove that it was my doing?"

We were quiet, both watching the traffic as we made our way up the 405. There was no way this could be scientifically tested. Stymied again.

Three days passed before I heard from Fred Branstein again.

"I found Lydia Martin," he said.

"Lydia? What about Carl?"

"He'll show up. Lydia's in the hospital. She's got the big C."

Cancer! Guilt rose up and slapped me in the face when I remembered how tired she looked the last time I saw her. For the last few days, I had cursed Lydia and Carl and wished them the worst. Now the worst had happened.

"Where is she?"

"At UCLA, undergoing some tests. I guess they opened her and decided it had gone too far. They just closed her up again."

"Is she in pain?"

"Dunno. I haven't seen her. I just got the word from a cute little surgical nurse I know."

I thanked Fred and hung up to think about what to do next. Quiet contemplation was what I needed. Suddenly, I was desperate to hear David's voice.

Although the day was crisp and overcast, I donned sweats and a windbreaker so I could walk on the beach. I headed toward my favorite spot to sit among the rocks about a mile up the shoreline. When I reached it, my only companions were a few seagulls with their necks tucked into their ruff, the wind disarranging their feathers, and a couple of sandpipers braving the elements to chase the waves back into the sea, looking for sand fleas or whatever it is they eat. The gulls stared at me until they figured out I had no food for them, then transferred their attention to the horizon.

I spread the blanket I'd brought and sat on the cold sand, sheltered from the worst of the wind by two black rocks. Closing my eyes, I imagined myself back in that space between spaces where I had first met my angel. Sure enough, David was there to greet me.

He opened his arms and I fell into his waiting embrace, feeling sheltered and safe. "*Welcome, my friend,*" he said, hugging me. Then he held me at arm's length and looked deep into my eyes. *"What bothers you, Paxton?"*

I took a deep breath and began. "Just about everything, David. I can't keep up this façade much longer. I'm not so sure the new Paxton Michaels is the real me."

David smiled. *"There is only the Paxton Michaels you create and no other."*

I felt like slapping him, and he knew it. He ducked, playfully, and stepped back. *"Why do you resist that which you are?"*

Mortified, I began to cry. "And just what am I? A freak? I can't stand people fawning over me like I'm some kind of guru. At the same time, others practically hold their fingers up in front of my face in the symbol of a cross, like I'm bad voodoo or something. Most of the time, my own daughter thinks I'm crazy. Which of these is the real me?

At least, David had the courtesy to look sympathetic. *"You're all of them, Paxton. You're the one who comforts the seekers with your knowledge of Spirit. You shock those who are close-minded. And Alex is simply trying to get used to having a mother who appears to have changed."*

"I have changed, David. I loved being a housewife and mother. At least, I thought I did. Now, I doubt that I could ever go back to being the good little woman who did everything she was supposed to do. I enjoy knowing that I have a new-found strength and that I don't have to have a man in my life to make me complete. At the same time, I don't feel like the dynamo Carl and Lydia Martin want me to be up on stage. Despite having spoken in front of thousands of people, I'm still terrified every time I stand behind a lectern. If I ever had to get out from behind it, the audience would see my knees shaking. I don't want to be a lecturer, going around the world talking to people I don't know and, for the most part, don't want to know."

David motioned for me to walk with him. When I first met him, this was how we carried on most of our conversations, strolling along side-by-side.

"No one ever said you had to lecture the multitudes," he reminded me.

"I know. But you charged me with getting your message out to people without telling me how to do it. Then the Martins came along and I figured they could help."

"You still have the power of choice, my dear friend. You can change that any time you decide."

We walked along in silence for a few minutes. Then I asked, "What about healing, David? Do I have the power to heal people?"

"I don't know. Do you?"

Feeling defensive, I said, "Well, I know it's not me who could do it. If anything, it would be God working through me." I looked at him for confirmation. "Right?"

"Not exactly."

That certainly surprised me. "What?"

"Remember, it is also the belief of the person you touch that is a determining factor. It is God working through him or her, as well as through you. You might be the catalyst, but you do not heal."

I could accept that. In fact, it was a huge relief to know that I didn't have some superior power that might send me off in a different direction to another place I didn't really want to be.

"Then I shouldn't pursue this thing that Lydia and Carl created, I guess."

"It is your choice," he said. *"As always."*

I rolled my eyes at the not unexpected answer. "I have to ask this anyway. Will you tell me what to do about the Martins?"

"Of course not. I know you will do what is right for all concerned."

I shook my head in disbelief. "David, I depend on you to tell me what is right. Can't you help me out just a little?"

He laughed. *"You already know, my friend."*

A cold nose against my hand startled me out of my meditation. The nose was attached to a black cocker spaniel with sandy paws. A woman's voice called, "Peggy, come here!"

Peggy ignored her mistress and begged me to pet her, which I did.

"I'm sorry," the woman said. "She's curious, friendly, and quite a pest."

I could have been miffed because the dog interrupted my reverie, but I don't think David had much more to say anyway. I rose, folded my blanket, and walked along beside Peggy and her owner.

"I'm Charlotte Dubin," she said. "I think we're neighbors. At least, I've seen you on the beach a few times. You live in the house with the big deck, don't you?"

"Yes. And I do believe Peggy and I have waved at each other a few times when I pass your place. I love the way she stands on her hind legs to peer over your railing. It actually looks like she's signaling to me with her paws at times."

Charlotte reached down to scratch behind Peggy's ears. "She's an old dear. I don't know what I'll do without her."

Puzzled, I asked, "Why? Is she ill?"

"Just old, mostly. It's unusual for her to romp like she is today. She has arthritis so bad, and I think she's in a lot of pain. Aspirin seems to help a bit. That's what her vet recommended. But she doesn't climb up beside me on the couch anymore, because it hurts when she jumps down." She stopped walking. "Well, here we are. Maybe I'll see you again."

"I hope so, Charlotte. It's been nice meeting you." I bent down and held Peggy's face between my hands. "And you, too, Peggy." She looked up at me with trusting, brown eyes.

I felt an electric jolt pass from me to the dog. Peggy yelped and sat down suddenly.

"Oh, what did I do? Did I hurt you?"

Charlotte dismissed the thought. "She often does that. She'll turn her body a certain way or lift her head a little too high. It wasn't you." She lifted the dog into her arms. "Come on, you old dear, I'll carry you the rest of the way."

We said goodbye again and I jogged the rest of the way home. Once there, I found the problem with the Martins hadn't gone away. Jay had called and left a message. *Carl Martin took a flight to Mexico last night. We may never see him again. I found his bank, but when I called to ask if they would cover a thousand dollar check, the answer was 'no'. I imagine he cleaned out the account.*

Would Carl do that to Lydia? My instincts told me he wouldn't desert her. Then I remembered that they had opened a trust account in Alex's name. I had sent them a hundred dollar check to open the account. Had they added to it? I searched through my files and found the account number that I had had a hard time getting out of the Martins. The bank representative said there was seventeen dollars left in the account and that I should try to bring the account back up to a hundred to avoid draining it with fees. After hanging up the telephone, I showered and dressed, and took a little ride to UCLA.

CHAPTER TWENTY-FIVE

THE FINAL DECISION

PARKING WAS A bear at UCLA. I drove around the covered lot for ten minutes before I found a vacant space that wasn't labeled Handicapped or Doctors Only. I finally followed a white-haired woman to her car and waited until she finished a phone call on her cellular before backing out. I decided that I had bad parking karma and resolved to work on the issue.

After several wrong turns, I found Lydia's room. Her eyes were closed when I entered, and I stood there watching her for a few minutes. She didn't look like the ogre I had made her out to be these past few days. Instead, she simply looked like a tired old woman with an IV running into her left arm. She was hooked up to monitors that beeped. Machines with numbers and graphs lighting up the screen made no sense to me, but must to her caretakers. Outside the room, several nurses discussed their Thanksgiving plans. It always amazed me that people came to a hospital expecting to rest, but were subjected to more noise and interruptions than they'd ever experience at home.

Lydia seemed to sense my presence and opened her eyes. I expected her to be surprised, but she just smiled a weak little smile. "Hello, Paxton."

"Hi, Lydia. I heard you're sort of down and out."

"Well, I hurt like hell where they sliced into me, that's for sure." A tear slid down her cheek. "Did Carl tell you I might not be around much longer?"

"Don't talk like that," I said. "You can get well if you want to."

She huffed a little and coughed. "That sounds like you really believe all those things you've been saying."

I was astounded. "Why, of course I do. I couldn't go around talking about them if I didn't."

She seemed a little more alert now. "Sweet girl, don't you know that people do that all the time? They'll say anything if it draws a crowd. And you certainly do draw a crowd."

"But honestly."

"Push that button for me, will you?" I did, and the head of her bed raised her into a sitting position. "Honestly, hmm? So you're saying that you actually think you spoke with an angel."

I did my best to keep the fury from my voice when I replied. "All this time, you and Carl didn't believe a word I said, did you? You thought I was making it all up just to make a buck."

"Well, yes."

"Then how is it that I have less than twenty dollars in the trust account that you and Carl set up for Alex? That was supposed to house the profit from my speaking engagements. What happened to the ten thousand from the Anaheim talk?"

Lydia lost her composure for the first time since I'd met her. "W-w-we had expenses."

"Ten thousand dollars worth of expenses? For what? Can you itemize them for me?"

She broke down then, lowering her face into her hands and sobbing. What was I doing, badgering a dying woman? I went to her bed and sat on the edge. Carefully, so as not to dislodge the IV, I took her in my arms and patted her as I would a child. "There, there, Lydia." We rocked back and forth while she cried and I patted. I began to wish that I had those healing powers that the Martins had invented. Maybe, if I could get her to believe…

"Lydia?"

She dried her eyes on the backless gown she wore. "What?"

"What would you do if you got well?"

"I'm not sure what you mean."

"If you were healed of this thing that appears to be attacking your body, and if there was absolutely nothing to restrict you, what would you do? How would you change your life?"

She didn't hesitate. "I'd move back to Atlanta. I hate Los Angeles."

"Then while you're here in the hospital, why don't you visualize all the things you'll do when you get there. Imagine where you'll live, where you'll shop, who you might meet, and so on. Think of the fun you'll have. Picture Carl as a country gentleman."

She laughed. "Not that last part; Carl would never be a country anything. He's a city person."

"Will you do it, though?"

She shrugged. "I suppose it wouldn't hurt. If nothing else, maybe Heaven will look a little like Atlanta. I can imagine that."

I took both of her hands in mine. "Look, Lydia, I could take you and Carl to court for bilking me out of the money I've earned. I don't believe you can justify enough expenses to entitle you to have spent every cent of it. However, I never intended to make any money from what I did, although it would have been nice to throw a little my daughter's way. I'm not going to sue you. And I'm not going to see you again. I'm terminating our contract, and I'll send you a letter to that effect. I'll find another way to tell the world what I know. In the meantime, I choose to see you as a healthy person. If you want this for yourself, then so be it."

When I said those words, I felt energy surge through me and out my fingertips into Lydia's weakened body. Her eyes widened. "Wha-what was that?"

I simply smiled and left. On the way home, I stopped to see Moira at her office.

"Well, bless me, speak of the devil and there you are," she said.

"You were speaking of me? To whom?"

"Your lovely daughter."

"Alex?"

"Mm hmm. She called here wanting to talk, so I let her bend my ear for a while. Guess she's been having some second thoughts about her mama."

"Oh?" I felt apprehensive. "Meaning what?"

"Don't look so scared, babykins. It's good news. She's been talking to that weird woman you met up in Berkley. Veronica. Seems the woman has persuaded your little girl that maybe you're not so crazy after all. She asked me how to approach you and say she's sorry for having doubted you. I told her to write you a letter. Sometimes it's easier to put things on paper."

Tears collected at the corners of my eyes. "Wow. I can't wait to check my mail."

"Oh, it'll be a while, I'm sure. She'll probably have to think about it some more, get the right words down in black and white, you know. Basically, I'd say the girl is growing up."

"Wow," I repeated.

"Now, honey child, tell Moira why you're here. This doesn't feel like a standard drop-in visit to say hi or let's go shopping."

"You're right. I just want to talk a bit. Do you mind?"

"Listening is what I do best. I'll put on the coffeepot."

I couldn't help smiling, because Moira's listening usually had her chomping at the bit to give advice, regardless of the subject.

I followed her to the kitchen and watched as she ground dark-roast beans and put them into her Mr. Coffee ®. When it began to sing its perking song, she sat down at a glass-topped table in her breakfast nook and patted the seat beside her. "C'mon, sit. Talk. Let Moira make it all better."

I took a deep breath and began. "I've made some big decisions today. For one thing, I know I'm not cut out to be a circuit speaker. I don't want to do it, and I can't reach as many people as I thought I could that way.

"My life is really great right now. I've learned to like myself as an individual instead of an extension of Robert. I loved being married, at least in the beginning, and maybe someday I'll marry again. But right now, I'm content to be alone."

For once in her life, Moira kept quiet and really listened while I talked.

"I got a phone call from a gallery in Santa Monica and took some of my artwork down there the other day. They asked me to prepare a one-woman exhibit. I'll have to spend quite a bit of time in front of an easel to finish the number of paintings they want for the show, but I have until March to do it. I can't wait to show you what I've been doing. It's so different from what I did before. It's like I was a pastel sort of person when I was with Robert. Now, I'm a bright rainbow of color. It's like comparing a black and white movie made in the forties to a DVD filmed today. And I'm good!

"I've also decided not to pursue any remedy with the Martins. I'm just getting out from under their influence."

Here, Moira almost broke her silence, but I held up my hand. "I've decided." She sank back into her chair and nodded.

"I've come to believe that there is a Divine Presence that is both "out there" and within me. I accept that It, whatever it is—intelligence, love, wisdom, creative energy—is expressing uniquely through me, and I am important to its fulfillment. I'm certain, because I have seen it work in my life, that I can develop my world however I choose to create it, if I am diligent in the process. Every thought, word and deed is cause unto its own effect, and I can be the one to decide what effect will come into being. Before David came into my life, I thought I had no control over what happened to me and gave my power away to Robert, to Alex, to circumstances and situations. Now I know who I really am, a spiritual being having a human experience, and I live my life by choice. I also have no doubt that every person on this earth can do the same.

"I'm going to write a book about my experiences. Somehow, I know this is the way I can reach the most people. I'll buy a laptop that I can take anywhere. Maybe I'll write at home, or on the beach, or up in Berkley, visiting Alex. It may take me a year, but when I'm done, everyone who picks up my story and reads it will know they have a choice on how they spend the rest of their lives."

When it was obvious that I had finished my little speech, Moira asked, "What about healing?"

"I'll never be able to prove it, yea or nay. If it's there, I'll get a chance to do it. If it isn't, it won't matter. People can heal themselves."

"Have you talked to David about this?"

"Not yet, but somehow, I don't think I have to. I believe I already have his approval."

Later, I did call on David. The conversation was brief.

"I'm going to write a book, David. Then, when I'm finished, people can read it and make up their own minds. They will either believe or not believe. It's their choice."

"That's all we ever wanted, Paxton. You've done well."

"But David, we never got to the second lesson."

"There is no second lesson, Paxton. There is only the one."

I experienced shock. "What do you mean, there's no second lesson? I can't tell people there's only one thing they have to learn. Moses had trouble with ten!"

"Why would you wish to complicate things? Truly, there is only one lesson."

"But we talked about so many things."

"All part of the first lesson. Think about it. Every question you asked, every bit of wisdom that was revealed to you, no matter how you received it, all had to do with choice."

"One lesson, huh?"

He nodded and began to fade from my sight. Suddenly I was filled with fear that I'd never see him again. "Wait! I love you."

"I love you, too, my friend."

The next morning, I sat down in front of my new computer and started to type.

It began on a typical, rather ordinary day.

THE END

EPILOGUE

I FINISHED PUTTING my story down on paper last night. When I wrote *The End*, I knew it wasn't. At the same time, I felt awed.

"I wrote a book!" I said. "I actually wrote a book." Whether or not you anyone believes what I have written doesn't really matter. *I* know the truth and have been transformed by it.

After breakfast this morning, I decided to take a walk on the beach. The sun had barely risen, and fog still shrouded the water. I could see only a few feet in front of me and, as I left footprints in the wet sand, I imagined being cocooned in the misty cloak, waiting for the sun to rescue me from a life of indistinct patterns. In the distance, I watched Charlotte Dubin, my neighbor, cavort with her dog. Peggy romped, jumping and playing like a puppy. This must be one of her good days, I thought, although I had noticed that she'd been having a lot of good days lately.

I felt sad. It had been weeks since David had come to me, even in a dream. I had wanted to ask his advice about some of the things I put down on paper. Apparently, the book was to be mine alone. If only I could see him one more time.

Suddenly, I did see him. He was walking toward me, barefooted, dressed quite ordinarily in a pair of cutoffs and a gray sweatshirt. "David!" I yelled, and ran toward him. He waved, but looked hesitant.

I threw my arms around him. "David, it's so good to see you. Where have you been?"

He spontaneously returned my hug, but just for a moment. Pushing back, he said, "Excuse me, have we met? I'm sure I'd remember you if we had."

Something was wrong. This was my angel. Wasn't he? I recalled David saying that he had taken the form of my ideal soul mate. Was this what he meant? That he actually had a human counterpart? The poor man must think I'm an idiot.

"I'm sorry. I-I thought you were someone else. You look just like him."

He laughed. "I think I'm sorry I'm not him. I like being greeted with such enthusiasm. Is he a good friend?"

"A very good friend. But I haven't seen him in a long time." Suddenly, I knew that I wouldn't be seeing David again.

"Do you live around here?" the stranger asked.

"About half-a-mile back down the beach. And you?"

"I live in West Hollywood, but I'm looking for a house to buy near here. I might end up being your neighbor if I can find just the right place. I'm a writer. I've been feeling the need to get out of a high-traffic area and live where I can instantly touch the hand of God when I need to. And the Pacific shore is the place where I can do that the easiest."

"We have something in common then."

"Great. Maybe there's more. Is there a possibility that you might have a cup of coffee with me? And maybe lunch?

If you're afraid to run off with a stranger for a couple of hours, I'm sure I can find someone to vouch for me."

I wasn't afraid. My angel had already vouched for him.

"By the way," he said as we strolled together on the wet sand, "how did you know my name is David?"

Los Angeles Times
April 7, 2017

TALENT AGENT SUES HOSPITAL

Lydia Martin sat quietly beside her husband and listened to the testimony of her former doctor, Eliot B. Ellis, who attempted to explain that he had correctly diagnosed Martin's cancer as terminal. Martin is suing for seven million dollars, alleging that Ellis's diagnosis forced her to submit to surgery when there was nothing wrong.

ABOUT THE AUTHOR

Barbara Harrison is a freelance writer, who has published many short stories and articles, as well as a self-help book titled ***15 Seconds to World Peace.*** She recently moved from Southern California and now lives in McKinney, Texas. If you want to let her know how you liked her book, you can leave an Amazon review, or email her at authorbarbaraharrison@yahoo.com.

Made in the USA
San Bernardino, CA
17 August 2018